MW00449680

MISSOURI OUTLAWS

MISSOURI OUTLAWS

BANDITS, REBELS & ROGUES

PAUL KIRKMAN

THE
History
PRESS

Published by The History Press
Charleston, SC
www.historypress.net

Copyright © 2018 by Paul Kirkman
All rights reserved

Front cover, top left: courtesy Library of Congress: LC-USZ62-3855; *top center*: courtesy
Wikimedia Commons; *top right*: courtesy Missouri Valley Special Collections, Kansas City
Public Library; *bottom*: courtesy Wikimedia Commons.
Back cover: courtesy Library of Congress: LC-DIG-det-4a20068; *inset*: courtesy Library of
Congress: LC-DIG-ppmsca-40662.

First published 2018

Manufactured in the United States

ISBN 9781625859150

Library of Congress Control Number: 2017960104

Notice: The information in this book is true and complete to the best of our knowledge. It is
offered without guarantee on the part of the author or The History Press. The author and
The History Press disclaim all liability in connection with the use of this book.

All rights reserved. No part of this book may be reproduced or transmitted in any form
whatsoever without prior written permission from the publisher except in the case of brief
quotations embodied in critical articles and reviews.

To Bill and Kay Kirkman

CONTENTS

CONTENTS

INTRODUCTION

I was born in Colorado and spent most of my youth in Kansas, but I have lived in Missouri some forty years now. It has taken time to understand this place. From the weather to the politics, Missouri is volatile and unpredictable. It is farm country, with lots of rivers and springs and good bottomland; but much of it is hill country with thick woods and rocky slopes. The sparsely populated Ozarks surround Branson, country music's second home, a little town overcrowded with thousands of tourists, theaters, stars and ex-stars. St. Louis and Kansas City bookend the east and west sides of the state, respectively, each brimming with people living urban and suburban lives free of country accents and bib overalls. Tiny towns with populations tallied in dozens, as well as several towns that measure in the thousands and tens of thousands, dot the state. Missouri is not just one thing or people. There is a culture, a character here that is both friendly and taciturn. We can't even agree on how to pronounce our own name; it is "Missour-eee" or "Missour-uh," depending on where you live. A wild frontier at the beginning of the nineteenth century, Missouri grew up in the golden years of westward expansion. Trails teeming with immigrants' wagons stretched the state's reach out to Santa Fe, California, Oregon and Colorado. The wealth of western farms, ranches and mines was funneled back to the East Coast and beyond. I have been sorting it out for myself over time, and I think this book will at least point the way toward understanding part of Missouri's role in the shaping of American culture.

When I was relatively new to the state, I saw a bumper sticker on an old pickup that read, "I'm from Missouri, and I will shoot you." I remember asking a friend who grew up here what it meant. He said, "Quick, name the two most famous people you know from Missouri." I thought about it, and he grinned as I came up with Jesse James and Harry Truman. He said, "One robbed trains and the other dropped atomic bombs....We aren't the sort of folks you want to play chicken with." It is true that from its difficult entry into the Union and throughout the nineteenth century, Missouri and Missourians developed a reputation for stubbornness (the state animal is the mule), pragmatism (it is, after all, the Show-Me State) and outlawry (far more than just the James Gang). To be fair, the majority of Missourians have been and are peaceful, law-abiding citizens, but a review of the facts (and the fiction) makes clear why nineteenth-century Missouri was labeled the "Outlaw State."

My original inclination when considering how to tell the story of the outlaws was to start from the vantage point of the state's remaining nineteenth-century jails, and you will still find that thread running through the book. In 2009, I was given the opportunity to help Jackson County Historical Society archivist David Jackson research and write a history of the 1859 jail and marshal's home in Independence. That project taught me how intertwined the local jail could be with a community's development and history. William Faulkner explored the depth of this sentiment in *Intruder in the Dust*:

> *It was old, built in a time when people took time to build, even jails, with grace and care and he remembered how his uncle had said once that not courthouses nor even churches but jails are the true record of a county's...a community's history, since not only the cryptic forgotten initials and words and even phrases cries of defiance and indictment scratched into the walls but also even the very bricks and stones themselves held, not in solution but in suspension, intact and biding and potent and indestructible, the agonies and shames and griefs with which hearts long since unmarked and unremembered dust had strained and perhaps burst.*

In dozens of Missouri communities, the old county or city jail still stands watch over streets where pioneers drove their wagons, where blue and gray armies spilled their blood and where sheriffs and outlaws faced off with six-guns blazing. Each is a testament to a time and people apart, a place that scarcely resembles the state we know today. Built in Missouri's first century, these buildings were a response to the needs of a society that grew up as the line of frontier moved west. Everything from minor infractions to riots, war and murder became attached to these buildings. The old marshal's home and jail on the Independence square is one of those survivors. The steel doors and stone walls compel the senses to a more personal awareness of the place's storied past, where one can touch the cells and breathe the air and feel the closeness of it all. Still, it is the people as much as the place that we want to know. Other lives, other people we can judge or emulate, empathize with or revile help to give meaning, color and context to a place and time. The sheriff who cleaned up a town, the bad guys he fought, the stalwart citizens who backed him up or turned their backs—this is the stuff of legend. And legend is the part of history we tend to hold dearest. I don't discount the many empty cells in want of a prisoner, the trains that successfully delivered the payroll or the thousands of quiet nights that saw no gunplay, but history in the telling is big, even if its parts are small. There is a big story in the making of the Outlaw State, and to convey it I had to choose some way to contain it. The nineteenth century is not the perfect vessel, but it is a good one for my purposes. I will spill a little over into the next era in the last chapter, but I will try to keep most of this story within its confines.

I must admit that I didn't pick this topic out of a hat. The subject of my senior thesis was the notorious characters of the Missouri/Kansas border. I even took a class on social outlaws in American history at the University of Missouri in the early 1980s. It goes back further than that, though. As a kid, I used to enjoy watching old Westerns on television with my dad. The heroes were always larger than life, and the bad guys always lost in the end. The characters often were named after real people, and as I grew up, I wanted to know more about them. The border of Kansas and Missouri was truly fertile ground for growing larger-than-life outlaws and lawmen. There was a twenty- to thirty-year period in the middle of the nineteenth century that found some of the best-known characters in American history living along that line of fire. Wyatt Earp, Wild Bill Hickok, Frank and Jesse James, Buffalo Bill Cody, George Armstrong Custer, John Brown, Calamity Jane, Belle Starr, William Quantrill, the Dalton brothers and many more left their mark or traced their roots to that blood-soaked ground. The Border War, the fight over slavery, gave the area a head start on the Civil War and tore Missouri apart. So many of those who made up the upper class before the war found themselves disenfranchised and financially ruined after. Outlaws like Cole Younger (whose father was a state senator) and the James brothers (whose father was a successful farmer and preacher) found fame and claimed vindication by attacking institutions run by their former enemies.

There was no shortage of sympathetic supporters for the former Rebels who "took back" from the railroads, banks and "carpetbaggers." Newspapermen like John Newman Edwards (a former adjutant to Confederate general Joseph O. Shelby), as founding editor of the *Kansas City Times*, compared the former rebels to Robin Hood. In *Noted Guerrillas, or the Warfare of the Border*, he wrote of the James brothers: "They have more friends than the officers who hunt them and more defenders than the armed men who seek to secure their bodies, dead or alive." Families who lost fathers and sons to the lost cause, who lost homes and land to the new order, could strike back at the victors vicariously through the outlaw gangs, and many provided assistance for the gangs or withheld it from the lawmen and Pinkerton agents who sought to end their careers. This era and its spawn have been fodder for dime novels, pulp magazines, silent films, talkies, television shows and more for over a hundred years. The story of America, even that of Missouri, cannot be rightly told without it. Though much has changed, it is still the same land, and the people are still a unique breed. I have been fortunate enough to visit many of the old towns where some of the buildings, banks, jails and courthouses still remain; where you can see and touch and take in the feel of their storied past. I hope I can convey a sense of how special, how valuable they are and do justice to the men and women who lived on both sides of the bars. Enjoy.

1

FRONTIER ROOTS

The frontier experience has often been cited as the catalyst that produced a unique American character. Historian Frederick Jackson Turner stated: "To the frontier the American intellect owes its striking characteristics, that coarseness and strength combined with acuteness and inquisitiveness; that practical, inventive turn of mind, quick to find expedients, that masterful grasp of material things, lacking in the artistic but powerful to great ends; that restless, nervous energy; that dominant individualism, working for good and for evil, and withal that buoyancy and exuberance which comes with freedom—these are the traits of the frontier." Critics might find Turner's view romanticized, but it is difficult to see how the frontier experience could not have influenced the development of the character of Missouri's first generation. In 1800, Missouri was not yet a state or even a territory of the United States. As part of New France, it had been passed from French to Spanish control and back again, with Native Americans—as well as British and American settlers—vying for possession. Though Native Americans had lived there for thousands of years, Spain, France and England all had greater influence over the territory's destiny in the eighteenth century.

Political and military actions thousands of miles away would continually mold the character and nature of everyday life in Missouri. The Seven Years' War cost France its holdings in the Louisiana Territory, which it ceded to Spain. The Spanish, however, did not settle in large numbers. Rather, they set up military/trading posts and tried to govern the French and Native

American inhabitants living there. British expansion and control of the northern waterways after the war led to an influx of French residents from Illinois and other points east of the Mississippi into Missouri, swelling their numbers and influence in the area. French fur traders based in St. Louis added a more prosperous political class to the community. The American Revolution again rearranged the deck, with the Spanish trying to induce Americans to settle in Missouri on the hope that they would help defend it against any British incursions. Spain returned the area to the French in 1800 through the Third Treaty of San Ildefonso, but Napoleon's need for funds to pursue war in Europe led to the sale of the Louisiana Territory to the United States in 1803.

The Louisiana Purchase had the effect of creating many false hopes; the Spanish hoped it would create a buffer between their colonies in the Southwest and the British and American settlements. The French hoped it would keep the British out of the area until Napoleon could defeat them in Europe and pursue New World agendas at a later time. Thomas Jefferson hoped that it would serve as a place to resettle eastern tribes of Native Americans and provide a water route to the West Coast and beyond. American colonists hoped for everything from riches in mining and land speculation to simply owning a small farm they could afford. To these conflicting visions one could add abolitionists' hopes that slavery in the United States would stop at the Mississippi River or British hopes that America would fail to expand its presence in the fur trade and cede part of the territory to them.

Adding to the mix of peoples and agendas, American expansion into the South uprooted eastern tribes of Native Americans, pushing them into conflict with tribes that traditionally lived in Missouri. All of these forces came to bear on a sparsely populated frontier where neither law nor order had settled in to stay. The largest towns in Missouri at the beginning of the territorial period were St. Louis (built largely on the fur trade) and Ste. Genevieve (an older French agricultural community)—neither settlement could claim much more than one thousand residents, if that. There were thousands of Osage, Missouri, Oto, Sac, Iowa and Shawnee either living or hunting in the territory, easily outnumbering these small communities. The isolated societies there were tight-knit and led by small groups of elites who had greater fortune and occasionally greater education than their peers. The Spanish land grants and permissions to operate various businesses held by members of these local cabals were essential to their success. Fearful of losing their holdings and livelihoods, the old guard had to work with the new American government while working against new American competitors seeking opportunities to prosper at their expense.

The series of earthquakes that hit southeast Missouri in 1811, the War of 1812 and warfare with and among the Osage and Sac left the territory reeling as the economy suffered and population growth sputtered. The transition from territory to state was fought out hundreds of miles to the east in the courts and in Congress as the division over expansion of slavery farther west and into an area that extended far north was addressed but not resolved by the Missouri Compromise. Conflicts of global powers; regional strife; and economic, political, racial and cultural differences all played out on the edge of the new frontier, setting the stage for the state and the sort of characters it would nurture. Nineteenth-century Missouri was in many ways a powder keg. From the pressure, conflict and violence that marked its nativity would emerge an explosion of larger-than-life men (and women) of action.

Americans in the Missouri Territory had to face isolation, hostile and foreign cultures, physical peril and privation. The majority of early settlers were uneducated and suspicious of government representatives who came from a different social group or background than their own. In 1800, Daniel Boone and his family were counted among the Missouri Territory's residents. Boone, whose exploits had brought him great fame but little fortune, had run into endless troubles over land claims and property taxes in Kentucky. His son Daniel Morgan Boone had gone to Missouri to scout the area for a possible move and was enticed to relocate to the Femme Osage region by the promise of Spanish land grants and a chance at a fresh start. The elder Boone, who had very little formal education but was respected as a leader, was offered land and the position of "Syndic" (a sort of local judge and jury who would resolve criminal and civil cases as well) by the Spanish lieutenant governor Zenon Trudeau. Boone accepted and continued to serve in that position until the United States took possession of the territory. Near his son Daniel Morgan's cabin, he held court under a large elm tree they called the "Judgment Tree." Like many of Missouri's backwoodsmen, Boone was less concerned with the letter of the law than with fair and just decisions. The rough and rowdy characters of the area would come to him with their disagreements, and Boone would settle matters without forcing the disputants to travel great distances to the higher courts. Punishment often came in lashes, sometimes laid on by Daniel Boone himself. In one case, a defendant was accused of stealing a hog; in another, one rowdy bit another's ear off in a fight. These sorts of disputes were like grown-up versions of schoolyard quarrels; local officials like Boone had to earn a reputation for fairness and strength in order to control their constituents. Once accepted, these men would often be expected to command posses, the civilian militia and sometimes even regular troops.

The Spanish system put a great deal of power in the hands of a small number of these strong leaders. After the Louisiana Purchase, the United States appointed Captain Amos Stoddard commandant of upper Louisiana. In an attempt to facilitate the transition of power, Stoddard kept most Spanish-appointed administrators in place and tried to work with worried residents through the transition. In 1804, Missouri would be the starting point of Lewis and Clark's Voyage of Discovery into what was then relatively uncharted wilderness. The group passed by the Boones' property, though whether they visited with the old explorer before setting out on their own adventures is unclear. Both Lewis and Clark would later be appointed in turn to serve as governor of the fledgling territory; their accomplishments and military experience on the frontier made them more acceptable than other political appointees. Lewis would serve only two years, spending much of his time out of the state, while Clark would govern for seven years. He then spent sixteen years as superintendent of Indian Affairs in Missouri. Both men were aware of the Boone family, and Clark knew Nathan Boone and employed him as a guide and surveyor.

In 1807, Governor Meriwether Lewis appointed Daniel Boone justice of the Femme Osage Township. Boone, like many of the Americans who had received land grants from the Spanish, was struggling to retain them under American law. Despite his financial difficulties, the Boone name continued to be a draw to settlers. The stories of his exploits as hunter and explorer were told and retold; a 1784 biography by John Filson had spread through the colonies, was read back in England and was popular in French and German translations, as well. Romantic poets like Byron, Wordsworth and Coleridge were inspired to pen verse about him, and James Fenimore Cooper drew from Boone's saga to create his *Leatherstocking Tales*. The Boonslick region was named after a saltworks started by his sons, and the elder Boone never resided in Booneville or Boone County, but many settlers were drawn to the region by its name association with the old explorer. His sons were well known and became respected leaders. Men with military experience, Indian fighters and adventurers like the Boones had a political advantage with the people of the wild territory. Settlers wanted vigorous leadership and men of action in place to respond quickly to the many and diverse threats and challenges.

Daniel Boone. *Courtesy Library of Congress: LC-DIG-ppmsca-23155 (digital file from original item).*

How, from where and by whom the new territory would be governed was of vital concern in the period following the Louisiana Purchase. Initially, Missouri, as part of the District of Louisiana, was under the jurisdiction of Governor William Henry Harrison of the Indiana Territory. A majority of Missourians opposed this arrangement because of the great distance to the territorial capital and the lack of legal protection for the institution of slavery. (Most of the American settlers in the Missouri Territory had come from slaveholding states.) In response to the general dissatisfaction, Congress reorganized the territory in 1805, making St. Louis the capital of the Louisiana Territory. In 1810, author Washington Irving visited the area and described the town:

> *Here were to be seen about the river banks the hectoring, extravagant, bragging boatmen of the Mississippi, with the gay, grimacing singing, good-natured Canadian Voyageurs. Vagrant Indians, of various tribes, loitered about the streets. Now and then a stark Kentucky hunter, in leathern hunting-dress, with rifle on shoulder and knife in belt, strode along. Here*

"Judgment Elm," Nathan Boone's lawn in Femme Osage, Missouri, where Judge Daniel Boone held court. *Courtesy Library of Congress.*

and there were new brick houses and shops set up by bustling, driving and eager men of traffic from the Atlantic states. On the other hand, the old French mansions, with open casements, still retained the easy, indolent air of the original colonists; and now and then the scraping of a fiddle, a strain of an ancient French song, or the sound of billiard balls, showed the happy Gallic turn for gayety and amusement lingered about the place.

This was the territorial capital, with its diverse interests and frontier spirit, coupled with a hundred years of French and Spanish settlement and influence.

The first governor of the territory, James Wilkinson, spent much of his two years in office trying to arbitrate the conflicting groups' claims on land, trading and mining rights and political influence. One challenge he inherited was that the Spanish had made a habit of giving yearly rounds of gifts to the various Native American tribes that lived in the area. When the American government took possession, several tribes descended on St. Louis expecting the United States to give them similar treatment. Though the federal government still entertained ideas of reserving much of the territory for Native American use, the majority of settlers moving into the area wanted the land and its produce for their own livelihoods. In 1804, a group of Sac and Fox made war on the Osage in a dispute over hunting grounds. That same spring, five Sac and Fox warriors were angered by U.S concessions to the Osage. Thinking that the Americans feared their rivals, they attacked a settlement a short distance north of St. Louis on the Cuivre River, killing and scalping three men with the hope of improving their tribe's bargaining position. When one of the braves was captured, the authorities were stuck with balancing the cries for justice from settlers with the real possibility of war. The captured brave was pardoned by President Jefferson but killed in an escape attempt before the pardon reached Missouri. In 1804, Governor Harrison had negotiated treaties with Sac and Fox tribal leaders after allowing them to drink heavily before signing. The tribes gave up huge swaths of land for small yearly stipends and vague promises of protection and future trade. Some of the tribal leaders who had dealt with Harrison gave up far more than they were authorized to, and the tribes balked later at the lopsided deals. Wilkinson was caught in the middle, as settlers wanted to move into lands that the tribes felt had been obtained through deceit. Despite the many obstacles to consolidation of power, there was a steady drumbeat toward greater cooperation and connection with the American government, even though undertones of dissent and independence were sounded by powerful players, including Wilkinson himself.

The bad blood between the various Native American tribes and the Americans set the stage for even greater conflict in the years leading up to the War of 1812. Harrison continued to use questionable practices in negotiating treaties, including the Treaty of Fort Wayne, which sparked open warfare with the Shawnee. Known as Tecumseh's War after the Shawnee leader, the 1811 conflict bled over into the War of 1812, as many tribes sided with the British, even after the Shawnee were defeated. The cycle of shady deal making and treaty breaking, new demands for more land and then warfare would repeat itself in Missouri as in many western states. The Americans' push to expand would eventually sweep all the tribes, even the Missouri, from Missouri. Early efforts by the U.S. government to control settlement and enact trade relations with the Osage and other tribes in the area largely failed. Fur-trading companies lobbied against government competition, and squatters largely ignored agreements limiting settlement. Fort Belle Fontaine was built in 1805; Fort Madison and Fort Osage as well as several smaller forts were also built in the early territorial period. Forts and factories were erected ostensibly to increase trade with and provide protection for local tribes. In reality, they served to extend control over the natives by creating dependence and debt and placing military forces within their territory. The forts also served as shelter for settlers against raids by the Sac and other tribes allied with the British (a particular threat during the War of 1812).

Groups of Missouri Rangers (militia authorized and paid for by Congress for set periods of time) were formed to defend frontier communities against the British and their Native American allies. Nathan Boone was made captain of a group of Missouri Rangers in 1812. Boone's group assisted U.S. troops from Fort Belle Fontaine in building blockhouses and patrolling the northern frontier. His brother Daniel Morgan Boone would serve as captain of a second group of rangers involved in several battles and skirmishes. Even Daniel Boone volunteered to join the militia. At seventy-eight he was not accepted for direct service, but he was allowed to help at the forts and perform nursing duties for the sick and wounded. All able-bodied men were expected to enlist or assist the militia and rangers during the war, and they had many opportunities to do so, as there was small-scale warfare along the frontier throughout the war years. Even after the British signed the Treaty of Ghent ending the war, their native allies continued to fight in Missouri. At the Battle of the Sink Hole (1815), northwest of St. Louis near Old Monroe, eight rangers were killed and several others wounded in a confrontation with Sac warriors led by Black Hawk. Dozens of settlements along the frontier had livestock stolen, were burned out or suffered loss of life in the year that followed. The Boonslick region was hit hard in those days. Settlers had to fortify their homes, and women and teens pitched in with the men to stave off marauding bands of warriors. One group of warriors left a white settler hacked to pieces, arms and legs dangling from trees. Scalping and mutilation and the killing of livestock, women and children were all part of warfare on the frontier. Black Hawk's tribe of Sac continued to attack settlements in Missouri and refused to make peace until May 1816.

Law and order was of necessity a primary concern, and communities often built a jail before ground was broken on schools or churches. Communities feared the violent and anarchic nature of the frontier and were quick to recognize the need for a strong force to counteract it. In addition to crime and warfare, as a slave state, Missouri had additional laws and a different order to keep. Slavery had existed in Missouri long before Americans had moved there, but as many of the settlers had come from southern states, the practice spread steadily through the farms and communities along the rivers. Fear of escaped or simply rebellious slaves was a part of a slave owner's psyche. In St.

A scene on the frontiers as practiced by the "humane" British and their "worthy" allies / Wm. Charles, del et sculp, Philadelphia 1812. Painting by William Charles. *Courtesy Library of Congress: LC-DIG-ppmsca-31111.*

Louis, the "black code" was instituted in 1804 and revised in 1808, 1811 and 1818. (Laws against slaves drinking, mixing socially with whites or free blacks or testifying in trials against whites were a few of the restrictions put in place that show the nature of their makers' concerns.) Patrols comprising local volunteers reported to a sheriff or a constable and saw to it that the codes were enforced. Runaway or rebellious slaves appeared in court documents regularly during that era. The many small-scale wars with Native Americans preceding the U.S. expansion into Missouri had been experienced firsthand by many of the frontiersmen settling the state. The War of 1812, along with intertribal fighting (often financed and encouraged by foreign parties), fueled fears on isolated farms and in small and far-flung communities. A large, limitless expanse into which a criminal could disappear where lawmen could not easily follow was just another fact of early Missouri.

The variety of threats, real and imagined, was more than enough to motivate early Missourians to take precautionary action. The Spanish had built a number of small forts in Missouri, including Fort Don Carlos and Fort San Carlos, and it was not unusual for civilians to fortify a home in the community—for example, Cole's Fort in Boonville and Fort Zumwalt in O'Fallon. The first log jail and courthouse in Independence, Missouri, were built in 1827, within a year of the founding of the town. The log courthouse continues to serve the community as a museum. The jail, like so many from that era, burned to the ground. A description in the county court records indicates that it was built on a similar plan to the military blockhouse in use at various forts in Missouri (including Fort Osage). The jail had a stone foundation but was made of heavy logs, two stories high, with entrance by way of stairs to the upper story. The lower story, or "dungeon," was accessed by a trapdoor in the middle of the second-story floor and had just one twelve-by-eighteen-inch window with steel bars on it. These log jails weren't built as long-term housing for prisoners—justice in those days was swift. Fines, lashings or death by hanging or firing squad were common punishments for lawbreakers. (At Fort Osage, there was a punishment post for lashings in the center of the parade.) It was 1835 when Missouri finally outlawed whipping and the pillory as legal forms of punishment (exceptions were made even then for certain crimes committed by slaves). While waiting in jail, prisoners endured dirt floors, little or no light, inadequate heat or ventilation and minimal food—all sufficient to guarantee an uncomfortable stay.

The territorial period was marked by a rapid growth of population in the communities along the rivers. Immigrants needed supplies and land, and merchants in St. Louis were quick to receive the economic boost that the outfitting business brought. Land was a trickier commodity, though. Phony deeds, old Spanish grants and Indian lands were all for sale to the unsuspecting. Matters were complicated further because many of the earlier settlers hadn't completed all the steps necessary to make sure their claims were officially recognized and recorded by the Spanish authorities. With no official record, the new American authorities had to listen to case after case and try to sort out competing and false claims. Squatters would work public lands with the hope that they could purchase them if and when the government decided to sell. Speculators would buy deeds or forge them and plot towns where none existed (and sometimes never would). In the southern mining areas around Ste. Genevieve, Potosi and Cape Breton, the factions led by Moses Austin (father of Stephen Austin) and John Smith T (the *T*, for "Tennessee," was used to distinguish him from others sharing the common name) would fight for supremacy using all methods fair and foul. Smith T had made his initial fortune in land speculation and the ferry business. He had family and political connections in Tennessee and Georgia and the means to compete with Austin. He also had a reputation as a gunfighter; he

Punishment post at Fort Osage. *Author's collection.*

carried up to four loaded pistols and a dirk with him, and he was reputed to have killed anywhere from six to fifteen men in fights or duels. Smith had a floating claim (a type of land grant from the Spanish that was specific about the amount of land granted but that let the bearer choose the location at a later date), which he had used to claim mining rights next to Mine a Breton (which Austin was already mining on his 4,250-acre concession). Austin was chief magistrate of the court of common pleas there, but Governor Wilkinson backed Smith T (who had two brothers in the army and a brother-in-law who was a congressman) as a better potential ally. Wilkinson removed Austin and made Smith T chief magistrate of the court.

The area was filled with a rough and ready cast of characters, and the pistol, cudgel and dirk were considered standard equipment. It was described variously as an armed camp having a lawless element of "pistol toting banditti." According to Henry Brackenridge, the mining area included "some of the rudest and most savage of the uncivilized portion of society"; it was "a constant scene of warfare," according to Christian Schultz. Fights broke out at the drop of a hat and, with all participants being armed, would quickly become deadly. In 1807, Frederick Bates (secretary of Louisiana Territory and later governor of Missouri), describing conditions there, mentions a case in which one man literally clawed another's eyes out, leaving him blind. The court awarded the victim $102 as compensation. Smith T and Sheriff Henry Dodge opposed Austin, and they had the men and weapons to make the military authority forbear forcing the issue. When Smith T and Dodge were accused of being involved in Aaron Burr's conspiracy to carve out a western empire (including Missouri) in the Louisiana Territory, Dodge turned himself in, made bail, then sought out and beat up nine of the grand jurors who had indicted him in fistfights (the rest fled the area). Smith T simply pulled a pistol and refused to be arrested, and the local authorities decided it was in their best interest not to pursue the matter further. Smith T and his men attacked and tried to take over Austin's claim at Mine a Breton in 1806 but were repulsed. On another occasion, one of Austin's men shot Smith T with a rifle and then slashed him with a knife, but Smith T's men saved him, and he survived to sue Austin for attempted murder. The two fought both in and out of court for years, but by 1820, Austin had lost his holdings to Smith T and left for Texas. Smith T would continue to be a force in the mining district for years afterward. Missouri congressman James S. Rollins told of an encounter with Smith T at a hotel where they were both staying. Rollins was preparing to leave to give a pro-temperance speech when Smith T stopped him and offered him a drink. Rollins tried to refuse, but Smith T insisted. Rollins continued to resist, but Smith T pulled a gun and gave him the choice of drinking with him or fighting with him. Rollins had several drinks with Smith T then went on to give his temperance speech—inebriated, but alive.

Highborn and lowborn scoundrels abounded in the Missouri Territory. Most of the leading citizens had invested in Spanish land grants and speculated in various industries. The commandant in the Ste. Genevieve district, Major Seth Hunt, had sold Smith T one of his floating claims and then joined with Austin in trying to kick Smith out. Governor Wilkinson, who sided with Smith T and removed Hunt for the appearance of impropriety, was removed from office himself in 1807 after being publicly decried for abuse of power and misuse of his position. He was proven after his death to have been working for years as a paid agent for the Spanish and was likely involved in the Burr conspiracy. Wilkinson was summed up by historian Frederick Jackson Turner as "the most consummate artist in treason that the nation ever possessed." And Theodore Roosevelt said of him: "In all our history, there is no more despicable character." Politics and commerce were deeply connected, and leading members of society would often get caught up in disputes that would lead to bloodshed. In 1807, Joseph McFerron shot and killed William Ogle in Cape Girardeau. In 1811, Dr. Walter Fenwick was killed by Thomas T. Crittenden in a duel on Moreau Island below Ste. Genevieve. Not to be left out, John Smith T fought a duel in 1819 with Lionel Browne (a nephew of Aaron Burr) on an island across from Herculaneum in which Smith T killed Browne. A sandbar in the Mississippi near St. Louis known as "Bloody Island" got its name from the many duels fought there. The island was neither in Missouri nor Illinois and thus was considered neutral ground. In 1810, a charge of cheating at a card game led to a duel between Dr. Bernard Farrar and James Graham. Both were wounded, and Graham ultimately died from his wound. In 1842, Abraham Lincoln and Illinois state auditor James Shields met there in a dispute over several letters criticizing Shields in a local newspaper. Lincoln was given the choice of weapon. The taller, stronger Lincoln chose cavalry sabers and, in preparation for the duel, hacked through a tree limb hanging over Shields's head. Seeing Lincoln's advantage, the seconds successfully convinced both to withdraw and settle their differences peacefully.

State senator Thomas Hart Benton (who shot Andrew Jackson in an 1813 duel but later became a supporter and political ally) fought two duels on Bloody Island in 1817 against Charles Lucas (his political rival for territorial delegate). Benton was shot in the leg and Lucas in the neck in the first exchange. Benton could still fight but did not press his advantage at the time. After Lucas recovered, they met again, and Benton killed Lucas. Benton remained a senator for thirty years and was succeeded by Henry S. Geyer, who also shot a rival in a duel. Shortly after Missouri attained statehood, two of the legislators, upon leaving the session, got into a fistfight. Governor McNair tried to intercede, and Stephen Cole physically stopped him from breaking them up, warning the governor that his title wouldn't protect him from the combatants. In 1823, Missouri secretary of state Joshua Barton was shot and killed in a duel with Thomas Rector, who was killed two years later in a knife fight. Missouri congressman Spencer Pettis engaged in a duel of words in the newspapers with Major Thomas Biddle that ended with the men in an 1831 duel on Bloody Island. The firing distance agreed upon was a mere five feet, at which both men hit their mark. Both men were mortally wounded. Ordinary businessmen in towns small and large had to defend their honor or face social and financial consequences. St. Louis had more than its share of disputes over "honor," like that between William Tharp and William Smith. An argument escalated to blows when Smith attacked Tharp with a cane. When Tharp recovered, he went to Smith and challenged him to a duel. Smith refused. Not satisfied, Tharp responded by putting an ad in the *Missouri Gazette* publicly calling Smith out as a scoundrel, rascal and coward. The social stigma was too much for Smith to bear, and the two finally met. Tharp shot and killed Smith.

Gunplay was to many just that, a form of play, albeit a deadly one. Riverboat man Mike Fink was well known in frontier St. Louis. Fink was a tough keelboat man who had earned his reputation as a marksman, brawler, bragger and practical joker. Stories about his exploits rose to mythic proportions, and the limited historical data available puts him in a class with Davy Crockett. It is likely that some of the stories about him are true and that the rest "oughta be." Whether the stories were started by Fink or by others who knew him, they were a mix of myth and reality, and the actual was nearly as outlandish as the invented. Fink worked a hard job that either broke a man down or built him up. Those keelboat men who poled freight up rivers built strong backs and arms. Fink knew he was tough and had a reputation for letting everyone else know it, as well. Boasting and bragging was part of the riverboat men's culture. Mark Twain wrote in *Life on the Mississippi* about two keelboat men who were trying to out-brag each other with boasts of their fighting ability. The two loudmouths swaggered and swung fists in the air but kept backing away from each other, showing no real intention of fighting. Bob, the self-proclaimed "corpse maker," and his

DREADFUL FRACAS ATWEEN THE GINERAL AND THE BENTONS AT NASHVIL

Above: Political cartoon depicting a duel between Thomas Hart Benton and Andrew Jackson. *Courtesy Library of Congress: LC-USZ62-60873.*

Left: Missouri senator Thomas Hart Benton. *Courtesy Library of Congress: LC-DIG-pga-06376.*

Andrew Jackson was severely wounded in an 1813 duel with Benton. *Courtesy Library of Congress: LC-DIG-pga-06376.*

rival, the "child of calamity," were both suddenly attacked and thrashed by another boatman, "little Davy," who had heard too much talk and seen too little action. Twain knew that the braggarts and genuine tough guys were mixed together in that culture and that there were some (like Fink) who would happily back up their claims. For sport, Fink and his friend Bill

Carpenter would take turns shooting a tin cup off of each other's heads. The two men were always more than willing to enter into confrontations with all comers with fists or weapons for nearly any reason. Carpenter ultimately was killed by Fink in one of their shooting demonstrations, and Fink was shot and killed the same year, 1823.

Indian fighters, trappers, miners, riverboat men and squatters all added toughness and a unique culture to the Missouri mix. With life and limb constantly at risk, it is little wonder that the state's inhabitants would inherit a strength of character and conviction that can only form in a crucible. Missouri's first generation was made up of pioneers and survivors who saw war and mayhem as part of everyday life. The leaders they looked up to dueled and quarreled and sued one another constantly. Gambling, land speculation, dueling, knife fighting, slave trading, horse racing and drinking were all largely accepted pursuits. It was an accomplishment to stand out in such bad company, and a congressman or judge might have more than one notch on his gun and still be considered a respected leader and pillar of the community.

LOG LOCKUPS

The first jails in Missouri were blockhouses at the various forts built by the French and Spanish and local jails almost universally made of locally cut logs. Some of the colorful terms to describe these structures reflected the diverse heritage of those who settled here. The word *calaboose* comes from old Latin *cala* ("protected place" or "den") and *fodere* ("to dig"; one tense is *fossus*, the root word for "fossil"). *Cala foss* became *calboze* in Spanish, then *calaboose* in Creole and was adopted as such into English. The term *hoosegow* came from Mexican Spanish as *jusgao*, which meant "court" or "tribunal," which came from *juzgar* ("to judge"). The word *jail* was from old French *jaole*, derived from Medieval Latin *gaveole*, from Latin *caveole* ("cave" or "enclosure"). *Pokey* was English and came from a poke, which was a sort of yoke attached to a pole to keep domestic animals from escaping an enclosure. *Stir* comes from a Romany (gypsy) word for a thing that cannot be moved (*staripen*), also the root for the word *stasis*. The word *clink* is Dutch for "door latch" but is also the name of a prison in London, so it may have come from either or both. Whatever you called them, the early jails were built quickly, cheaply, soundly and with little concern for comfort.

Since so few log construction buildings from Missouri's territorial era have survived, historically accurate re-creations based on the original plans are a valuable tool for presenting these structures to the public. Built at the original location chosen by William Clark, the blockhouses at Fort Osage were reconstructed from original plans and look like a typical jail of that era. The Fort Osage National Historic landmark is located in Sibley, Missouri. Hours of operation are 9:00 a.m. to 4:30 p.m., Tuesday through Sunday year-round. American log structures tended to be constructed with logs laid out horizontally, while the French and Spanish tended to use vertical posts. Fort Osage combined the styles, with a stockade of vertical posts and blockhouses laid out on horizontal lines. Blockhouses were used as barracks, storage facilities, shops, defenses and jails depending on the needs of the day. If a blockhouse was used as a jail, modifications like iron rings to attach chains to and double walls or reinforced roofs and floors were added to reduce the risk of escape. Most early jails were built as a response to crime rather than part of a broad plan for settlement. The first jail in Johnson County was an overturned wagon bed. The first prisoners were placed inside the improvised prison under the supervision of a couple of guards. The prisoners supposedly convinced the guards to leave by offering them money to buy a gallon of whiskey for the group to share. When the sheriff came to check on the prisoners the next day, the guards were found passed out under the wagon. The prisoners were long gone.

Blockhouses at Fort Osage National Historic Landmark. *Author's collection.*

Though most wooden jails were more effective than Johnson County's makeshift coop, they were equally unsuited to meet a community's long-term needs. Wooden walls could be chiseled, sawed or burnt through. Chinking between logs could be loosened, and fire was an ever-present hazard. Few if any of these early wooden jails lasted past the midcentury mark. The log jail in Independence was two stories with a stone foundation and a double log wall on the lower story. Access to the building was by staircase to the upper story, while the "dungeon" was reached through a trapdoor from the second floor. Three small windows with iron bars in them (two upstairs, one down) were also included in the relatively well-thought-out plan.

The first courthouse in Independence was built within a year of the town's first log jail and used similar materials. The county court sat there for half a dozen years until a brick building was erected in the center of the town square. That second courthouse, though often expanded and renovated, was incorporated into the center of the current courthouse and is still in use. The old log building went through various incarnations, even serving as temporary offices for county official Harry Truman before he moved on to higher offices. In 1916, it was moved to its current location and made into a museum. The 1827 Log Courthouse in Independence, Missouri, is located at 107 West Kansas Street. Its hours of operation are Monday through Friday, 10:00 a.m. to 2:00 p.m. In Liberty, Missouri, at 216 North Main Street, a partial rebuild of the jail Joseph Smith and other Mormon leaders were kept

1827 Log Courthouse Museum in Independence, Missouri. *Author's collection.*

in is a museum owned by the Church of Jesus Christ of Latter-day Saints. Built on the original site of the old jail, the representation has a front façade with the back cut out for visitors to view the interior log building (outer walls were stone masonry construction, two feet thick). Museum hours are 9:00 a.m. to 9:00 p.m., Saturday through Sunday. Leaders of the Mormon Church kept in both the Independence and Liberty log jails had little good to say about the experience, mentioning the bad food and having to sleep on stone floors in dark rooms. These modern re-creations serve to remind us not only of past events but also of the need for preservation so that future generations can experience firsthand some of the structures and objects associated with various events in history.

2

TRAILS WEST

In 1800, for many, the thought of settlement beyond the Mississippi was a dream for distant generations. Trade with the Indians who were there and perhaps resettling some of the eastern tribes was as far as the U.S. government's thinking had progressed. By the time Missouri had attained statehood, the influx of settlers quickly pushed tribes well beyond Missouri's eastern border. The Boonslick area included settlements along a trail blazed by Daniel Boone's sons Nathan and Morgan Boone that led to a salt lick in Howard County, Missouri. The trail started west of St. Louis in St. Charles and ultimately extended about 130 miles to Franklin. Settlements along the trail would grow into towns that included Booneville (1810), Columbia (1818), Williamsburg (1824) and Fulton (1825). In December 1820, the state encouraged continued expansion by passing a bachelor tax of one dollar each for unmarried men between the ages of twenty-one and fifty. Farther west, small communities were forming as landings on the Missouri River became jumping-off points for settlers moving west, gathering places for trappers and homes to merchants who served as suppliers, buyers and shippers. Lexington was platted in 1822 and Independence in 1827. Eventually, the community at Chouteau's Landing (circa 1821) would grow up to become Kansas City. River traffic advanced with the expanded use of steamboats during this era, but the first of several shots in the arm for the state was the opening of trade with Mexico. Spain had denied or limited trade, but when Mexico won its independence in 1821 a golden opportunity arose. William Becknell lived on a farm near Franklin,

Missouri. In 1821, he set out for Santa Fe with $300 in trade goods, which he converted to $6,000 in silver coin.

His subsequent trips over the next few years were even more profitable, and Missouri would benefit immensely from the new trading partnership that formed along the western trail. Within a decade, trailhead towns like St. Joseph and Independence would be filled with the sounds of harness- and wagon makers, barrel coopers and various other suppliers of the needs of the bullwhackers and mule skinners who plied the trail with their wagons filled with trade goods headed for Mexico. The trade on the trail would average $200,000 per year from 1822 to 1843. In 1846, Francis Parkman, author of *The Oregon Trail*, wrote of Independence: "The town was crowded. A multitude of shops had sprung up to furnish the emigrants and Santa Fe traders with necessaries for their journey; and there was incessant hammering and banging from a dozen blacksmiths' sheds, where the heavy wagons were being repaired and the horses and oxen shod. The streets were thronged with men, horses and mules." The frenetic activity preparing the wagon trains would enliven the whole town.

In Franklin, at the eastern terminus of the Santa Fe Trail, a teenager by the name of Christopher "Kit" Carson would listen to the tales of adventure told by trappers, traders and mountain men; watch the wagons and mules roll by; and dream of running away from his apprenticeship to saddle maker David Workman. Carson's father was a Revolutionary War veteran who had moved the family from Kentucky to the Boonslick area. Kit's mother remarried after his father's death, and his stepfather had sent him to apprentice for Workman. Carson's older brother was married to Daniel Boone's great-niece, and their daughter Adeline was Kit's closest childhood companion. Kit grew up on the frontier, surrounded by people who had launched forth into the wilderness with guns and knives and carved out a place for themselves. Young Missourians of his generation were inevitably drawn to the trails and the West. In 1825, at the age of sixteen, Carson took off with a trading party on the Santa Fe Trail. His career path would include stints as trapper, guide, Indian agent and soldier. His rise to fame through a daring but difficult career was sparked by the excitement offered by life in the West. Neither the first nor last to be caught up in the allure of the frontier, Carson was just one of many of Missouri's young men who thrived on adventure and would pass a restless nature on to the next generation.

Fur trappers and mountain men, explorers and traders were pushing farther and farther west in the 1810s and 1820s. Men like Kit Carson, Jim Bridger and Zebulon Pike would travel over great swaths of the country

Kit Carson. *Courtesy Library of Congress: LC-DIG-cwpbh-00514.*

then return with larger-than-life stories of the adventures they had and the wonders they saw. The river routes had brought settlers down the Ohio, up the Mississippi and up the Missouri, but as the Missouri turned sharply north at the western edge of the state, the overland trails began. Blazed by trappers and traders, the various western trails converged at Independence, Kansas City and St. Joseph. The western boundary of the state was more than a line dividing frontier and civilization. In the 1830s, a number of Native American tribes had been "relocated" west of the Missouri line. Many tribes accepted annuities from the U.S. government as partial compensation for the lands they ceded. Just across the Missouri line, the town of Westport can trace its roots to trader John C. McCoy, who wisely built his store right on the state line in order to be the closest place for tribes to spend their annuities. In 1846, Francis Parkman described the trailhead town of Westport, which is now part of Kansas City: "Westport was full of Indians, whose little shaggy ponies were tied by dozens along the houses and fences. Sac and Foxes, with shaved heads and painted faces, Shawanoes and Delawares, fluttering in calico frocks, and turbans, Wyandottes dressed like white men and a few wretched Kansas wrapped in old blankets, were strolling about the streets or lounging in and out of the shops and houses." The political lay of the land as well as the topography of northwest Missouri would lead settlers once more to petition the government to push the Native Americans out of the area they had been "given" in exchange for the lands they originally inhabited. Thousands of settlers crossed the prairie heading to Oregon and California. In 1843, a wagon train of one thousand people left Independence for Oregon. Large groups heading for the Southwest and Northwest left each spring, and in 1849, hundreds of thousands passed through in a mad rush to California, where gold had been discovered on the land of former Westport trader and hotelier John Sutter.

As part of Jackson County, Westport was under the jurisdiction of the Jackson County sheriff. The first sheriff was Joseph Walker. He had been a trapper and mountain man who traveled extensively throughout the West. He was arrested in 1820 for trying to barter with the Spanish but, five years later, would lead a survey team to mark out the Santa Fe Trail to a much more welcoming Mexican trade. In 1828, the six-foot, two-hundred-pound Walker, who was known as a crack shot and a strong leader, was appointed Jackson County sheriff. His experience in the frontier and on the trails was considered more than adequate preparation and qualification for the job. Walker served for four years, including during the era of the Mormon eviction from Jackson County. Rather than serve a third term, he found a more lucrative job selling horses to trappers and ultimately ended up being a successful rancher in California. Walker's deputy, Jacob Gregg, would also serve as sheriff. Gregg had driven a team in the first wagon train to Santa Fe, served as the county's first surveyor and moved up from deputy to sheriff and, eventually, state representative. A southerner, Gregg owned slaves, and had made a comfortable living in farming, trade and public

Westport, Missouri, circa 1859. This is a depiction of old Westport with a cart headed west on the Independence road. *Courtesy Westport Historical Society.*

service. He had nine children and lived into his nineties. During the Civil War, Gregg's sons Frank and William H. rode with William Quantrill's guerrillas, being outlaws in the same county their father had served in and helped build. Years after the war, former outlaw William H. Gregg served as deputy sheriff of Jackson County. The same experience, daring and skill that would mark the careers of successful lawmen could also be found in their adversaries, and many would end up working both sides of the law. The temptation of quick money on the wrong side of the law, poor pay on the right and adventure in the lawless West led more than a few deputies and constables to break bad and turn outlaw. The chance to settle down and be in with the political and business crowd and move up in society convinced other men to leave the outlaw trail.

Both commerce and migration were tied to the many trails across and through Missouri. In the 1840s, the Oregon Trail would stretch from Independence to the Oregon Territory. The California Trail would also start in Independence and branch off into various "shortcuts" as pioneers raced to get land after the Mexican-American War and gold after the discovery at Sutter's Mill. In 1857, the Butterfield Overland Trail added stage service from St. Louis to San Francisco. Like the Pony Express (from St. Joseph to Sacramento), however, the looming Civil War and the rise of telegraph lines connecting the East and West made it a short-lived enterprise. There were cattle trails from Texas to Missouri. Northern and southern routes to California, military roads, old Spanish trails and Indian traces like the Osage Trace and the Shawnee Trace crisscrossed the state and stretched out into the West and Southwest. The forced migration of Native Americans under the Indian Removal Act of 1830 added the Trail of Tears black mark to the many routes that crossed Missouri. All the movement of goods, materials and people led to booming trailhead towns, financial opportunities in both legitimate and unlawful activities and a rising tide of migration, building and growth.

It's been said that "where there is an ocean, there will be pirates." The western trails stretched out of Missouri like sea routes from a coastal city. In the nineteenth century, the six hundred miles between Kansas City and Denver featured no large metropolitan areas. More than a century later, this is still largely the case. There are wide-open spaces not so far west of the Missouri border that even now make the wise pause to fill the gas tank, gather snacks and check the oil. In the trailhead towns, one could purchase big Conestogas, quality wagons (like those built in the Independence shop of former slave Hiram Young) and junk on wheels that would fail before the trip was half done. Small farm wagons or church buggies like the Dearborn weren't meant to bear heavy loads or undertake long trips over uneven terrain. Many of these lighter-weight wagons were seen abandoned by diarists who wrote of their experiences on the trails. With the lure of huge profits, swarms of guides, outfitters and experts of various kinds selling everything an immigrant could need descended on the trail towns. Though many sold legitimate products at exorbitant prices, there were plenty of purveyors of second-rate rigs, geriatric horses or mules and worn-out wagons. The con man, whether he was working the riverboats, the land office or the supply town, had a booming business in Missouri, and the stories of how people got fooled slowly worked their way from initial anger or heartache to comic folklore. Mark Twain included a couple of these characters (the Duke and the Dauphin) in *Adventures of Huckleberry Finn* and managed to give them laurels for their clever capers and then a good tar and feathering for their villainy.

If an immigrant managed to get a good wagon, a good team of oxen, an experienced wagon master leading their group and sufficient supplies, there was still no guarantee that they wouldn't be attacked or robbed by outlaws, Indians or even other members of their party. Whether you were an immigrant heading west, a rancher bringing up cattle from Texas, a

Wrecked wagons were a common sight on the trails west. *Courtesy Library of Congress: LC-DIG-ppmsca-20088.*

settler building a cabin in western Missouri or a stagecoach driver out of St. Louis, you were a target, an easy mark for those who lived on the frontier and preyed on the commerce passing through. Crime statistics from the early years on the trails are sparse, but later in the century Wells Fargo reported more than three hundred stagecoach robberies and attempted robberies between 1870 and 1884 and nearly five hundred by century's end—and that's just one company. There were four drivers killed, two guards killed and ten wounded and four passengers killed and two wounded. The outlaws did not fare well, either. Five were killed during robberies, eleven died later at the hands of law enforcement and seven were killed by citizens (read "lynch mobs"). In a review of ninety-one accounts (diaries, letters and other correspondence) of travelers on the Oregon Trail, in 1852–53, there were twenty-three murders, one suicide and ten executions. One gang that had preyed on the trail trade was led by William McDaniel. He and gang member Joseph Brown were convicted of robbing and killing Jose Chavez, a New Mexico trader who had been traveling from Santa Fe to Independence. Other members of the gang managed to obtain pardons or face lesser charges, but McDaniel and Brown were executed.

In 1836, a penitentiary was built in Jefferson City, ostensibly to house some of the many outlaws who roamed the state. Governor John Miller had suggested the prison be built in Jefferson City, hoping it would help the town retain its position as the state capitol. The original prison had fifteen prisoners and only one guard. In the first few years, the majority of men were imprisoned for grand larceny. Few had murder charges, but theft of horses, forgery and the occasional stabbing were attributed to some of the early residents. In those days, few convicted of murder made it past the hangman's noose to stay in the pen (later known as "the walls"). Prisoners worked in a brick-making operation there in the 1830s. The first generation of Missourians was made up of frontiersmen and survivors who saw war and mayhem firsthand. The next generation was much more transient, as expansion and immigration led to rapid growth and change. Though many communities were established during this period, the constant flow of new people to and through the state made demographics and population centers more fluid. Both Independence and St. Joseph were bigger than Kansas City, and Jefferson City would have several contenders claiming to be more qualified to be the state's leading city. However, the capitol did not move, and the penitentiary stayed, as well, keeping its doors closed—and locked for operation until 2004. By the end of the nineteenth century, there were two thousand inmates behind "the walls."

The first wave of migration was from Border States like Kentucky and Tennessee. Along the Missouri River into the Boonslick area and beyond, southerners came, many bringing slaves with them. Quickly outnumbering the French and Native American population, these newcomers were mostly Scots-Irish Protestants. Though Americans from Illinois, Indiana and other northern states came as well, the majority of the first generation of Americans there was from the South and influenced by southern traditions. Though Missouri did not have the large-scale cotton production and concentration of slaves that many southern states did, the number of slaves grew steadily in communities along the Missouri River, marking the area as "Little Dixie." Communities like Boonville, Lexington and Liberty used slaves to grow hemp and other commodities less associated with traditional southern culture. Slaves in Missouri were more often owned in twos and threes rather than in dozens or hundreds, but the intimidation and control necessary to the institution required laws and attitudes that would influence not only those who owned slaves but also those who didn't. Patrols, slave hunters, whips and shackles came along with the justifications and prejudice that were necessary to keep a people in bondage. The wealthy and successful generally owned slaves, the rest either wished they did or kept their mouths shut about it, as even advocating abolition could mean severe financial and social repercussions. As slavery was a part of southern culture, it was part of Missouri culture and law. Removing it would prove devastatingly difficult.

In the 1830s, a second wave of immigration came from an unlikely source. In his mid-thirties, Gottfried Duden had spent three years in Missouri, chronicling his experiences and insights about everything from mining to slavery to duck hunting with Nathan Boone. On his return to Germany, he published a guide, compiled in a series of letters, for German immigrants extolling the state as a destination. Thousands read and followed his advice to move to Missouri and to do so in large groups for safety and to buy larger tracts of land communally. The first large group, known as the Berlin Society, arrived in 1832, and thousands more followed them as large German communities in the state naturally made it a more appealing destination to their fellow countrymen. By 1840, more than 38,000 Germans had settled in Missouri, and that number would more than double by 1860, as a second wave came in the early 1850s. The next largest group of immigrants came from Ireland. Starting in the mid-1840s, large groups of Irish began arriving in Missouri. Driven in many cases by the potato famine, many found work loading steamboats or laying track for the railroads. There were other groups from all over Europe, including a Jewish community in St. Louis, but the majority of Missourians came from one of the three main waves.

The combination of immigration to and emigration from other states or countries through Missouri contributed to the formation of the state's personality. In the Ozarks, there were clannish areas where outsiders were not easily integrated and even neighboring families could become involved in feuds. In the communities of Little Dixie, a distinct culture and politics as well as a slave economy came with the many settlers who hailed from the South. Along the Missouri and Mississippi Rivers, German communities like Hermann transplanted Old World culture, language and craft to re-create the familiar sights and sounds of Central Europe. The western trail towns like St. Joseph, Independence and Westport were built on trade and commerce from all directions. These towns grew up negotiating and connecting east and west, supplying immigrants and trading with Native Americans. They had to be open to new ideas and changing circumstances. The isolation of smaller communities spread throughout the state contrasted with the diversity and variety in the larger communities. There was no one Missouri, rather a jumble of cultures and norms. Travelers on the trails talked about "seeing the elephant" or experiencing the West firsthand—sometimes good, sometimes bad, but always bigger than life. Missouri was the elephant, too; someplace that had to be experienced, even though it could be dangerous. As the line of frontier moved west from Missouri, there was still a pause at its border that would last for decades. The western portion of the state would be tied to the frontier and serve as a safety valve for the pressures that expansion and change would bring. Missouri has been seen alternately as a place where hope starts and where civilization ends. It was said the Sabbath didn't exist west of the Mississippi, and yet the state has been fondly called the mother of the West. The frontier experience changed with the landscape as it moved west, but Missouri, from its roots to its branches extending along the trails, maintained a connection to America's constant renewal and expansion.

STONE STOCKADES

The log jail, even when carefully planned and built, had a number of flaws that led most communities to replace it within a few years with a more substantial stone structure. Besides the susceptibility to fires, both accidental and intentional, wood was easier to saw through, kick out or otherwise destroy than stone. Small stone calabooses were commonly the second jail in many communities. Sturdily built to withstand attempts from within and without to free their denizens, several of these old jails are still standing. Heavy stones locally quarried made escape more challenging for inmates. Iron bars and doors would be set in stone, and chains could attach the prisoner to a wall and floor if necessary. A window and perhaps a stove were used for temperature control in these newer structures. Built for swift justice and short stays, these stone jails generally had few cells and fewer prisoners. By 1838, the State of Missouri had built a penitentiary, where those who had committed heinous crimes could be housed for longer terms. Local jails still held prisoners for petty crimes and those awaiting trial and were visible reminders that lawlessness would not be tolerated. The stone calaboose ranged from one- and two-cell "drunk tanks" to two-story blockhouses. Some had separate entrances for the different levels. A ladder might be lowered into a dungeon area for the hardcore criminals, while stairs might lead to a more comfortable upper level reserved for female or younger

Shackles attached to cell floor in 1859 Jackson County Jail. *Author's collection.*

prisoners. These simple but effective structures were not built for comfort or long-term housing, but they were functional at keeping criminals separated from society until they could face trial and judgment.

Dozens of nineteenth-century stone "calabooses" remain in various parts of Missouri. At the Missouri state historic site and National Historic Landmark village of Arrow Rock, the stone jail (built in 1873) can be seen, along with several historic buildings. The historic site's office's hours of operation are 8:00 a.m. to 4:30 p.m. year-round. The town dates back to 1829 and was on the Santa Fe Trail. After the Civil War, the railroad bypassed the town, and nearby Blackwater was platted in anticipation of the new route it would take. A mock-up of Blackwater's old wooden jail with a period steel cell sits just off Main Street. Stone jails in Palmyra (Marion County; built in 1858), Elsberry (1896) and Vienna (Maries County; in use 1858–1942) are managed by local historical societies and can be viewed by appointment. In Rolla, a large stone jail is located at Third and Park. Built of dolomite blocks in 1860, it was used during the Civil War by the Union army for storage and to hold prisoners. After the war, the county billed the U.S. government and was paid fifty dollars a month for the two years during which the jail was "borrowed"; the jail was still in use until 1912. In Iron County, the stone jail that housed its first prisoner in 1867 is not only still standing but is also still in use as a county jail. The stone jail in Mokane was often used as a drunk tank; one of its first inebriated customers was the

Stone Calaboose, 1873, a popular site at the National Historic Landmark Village of Arrow Rock, Missouri. *Author's collection*.

Carondolet Courthouse and Jail, 1880. Emil Boehl, Photographs, P0825, 025438. *State Historical Society of Missouri Photograph Collection.*

Cole County Jail. *Courtesy Library of Congress.*

Hickory County Jail in Hermitage, Missouri. *Courtesy Library of Congress.*

man who built it. For years after the old stone jail was no longer used by the county, locals who had had too much to drink would use it to sleep their revels off rather than face the music at home. There are several of these old buildings that are not being used as jails or museums. In Farmington, the old St. Francois County Jail (built in 1880) is being used as a bike hostel, while in Palmyra, the old city jail (known locally as "The Calaboose") (circa 1875) has been repurposed as a restaurant and pub. Some of the old stone jails were torn down in their prime, while others served for a century and faced destruction because the space they occupied was needed. Still more just sit empty. In Hickory County at Hermitage and in Ozark County at Gainesville, old stone calabooses remain standing, their stories untold or forgotten.

3

THE LITTLE WARS

ut of the many minor struggles in Missouri's territorial period and first decade of statehood would grow larger conflicts that would lead Missourians to participate in a series of little wars in the following decades. The key conflicts over slavery, borders, Indian removal, cultural hegemony and trade led to another generation of Missourians having military and quasi-military experience, as the weight of fighting small wars fell on their shoulders. Missourians were involved in conflicts ranging from bloodless standoffs to town-destroying murderous battles. Military experience was commonplace at all levels of society. In the first decades of statehood, Governors McNair, Miller, Dunklin, Boggs, Price and Marmaduke all served in militia or regular army units. Their experiences ranged from putting down the Whiskey Rebellion, to fighting the British in the War of 1812, to serving in the Mexican-American War. McNair had also been a federal marshal, and Dunklin, who had owned a tavern in Potosi, simultaneously served as county sheriff and worked as a lawyer. Their experience was good preparation for leading the state in its tumultuous early years. In 1829, members of the Ioway tribe led by Big Neck had returned to their former hunting grounds in northwest Missouri in violation of a treaty. The group came into conflict with a group of settlers, and troops were sent for to move them out of the area. At Battle Creek, several members of Big Neck's tribe were killed, as were four members of the militia who pursued them. The Black Hawk War in 1832 once again spread fear of mayhem across the frontier, as two thousand militiamen were sent to patrol the border. (The war ended before Missouri troops became involved in the fight.) In 1836, the tiny Heatherly War again sparked fears of widespread warfare with Native Americans, but it ended up being quickly resolved with little bloodshed. In 1837, six hundred Missouri troops were tapped for the Seminole War. In the Battle of Okeechobee, forty men, including their colonel, were killed or wounded. That same year, militia drove the remaining Osage out of southwest Missouri in what was dubbed the Osage War. In 1839, a dispute over Missouri's border with Iowa Territory brought out militias from both states and led to what was dubbed the "Honey War"—tax agents from Missouri had cut down three trees with beehives in the disputed area to collect honey in partial payment of the taxes the Iowans refused to pay.

The 1838 Mormon War was the culmination of a conflict that began in 1831 as Mormon settlers flocked to Jackson County at the behest of their leader, Joseph Smith. Mormons were seen as a threat because of their support of abolition and unique religious beliefs. (In addition, Smith had prophesized that the Mormons would inherit the land from the other settlers there.) The Mormons were asked to leave the area by a mob of armed locals in October 1832. Forced from Jackson County, the growing population of Mormons in the state was shuttled off to northwestern counties with small populations, but conflicts over the group's growing political and financial power and religious beliefs led to attacks on and reprisals from the ill-treated newcomers. Dozens were killed and hundreds injured, and the state militia ultimately forced the group out of Missouri at gunpoint.

Several Missourians were involved in the settlement of Texas. Stephen Austin (known as the "Father of Texas") spent his childhood in Potosi and as a young man was a member of Missouri's territorial legislature. Half a dozen of the Alamo defenders hailed from Missouri, and many Missouri families had members who fought in the war for Texas independence. Between 1839 and 1841, the Slicker War raged in the Ozarks in Benton County, Missouri, as vigilante groups administered slickings (beating with hickory switches) to various wrongdoers. Vigilante and anti-vigilante groups formed and fought, and a number of the combatants were killed; some died from the slickings. The governor was forced to call out the militia to break up the groups. In 1843, clear across the state in Lincoln County, another vigilante group started its own slicker war against horse thieves, counterfeiters and other criminals. After two years of cleaning house, and a number of deaths, the group apparently felt it had done its job and disbanded. Vigilante and anti-vigilante groups became common in rural areas of the state and often included political and business leaders in their ranks.

In 1846, conflict with Mexico over Texas statehood led to the formation of General Stephen Watts Kearny's Army of the West. Missouri volunteers made up a large portion of the force that saw action. These troops participated in battles at Brazito and Sacramento, and Missouri volunteers totaling seven thousand men were involved in various actions throughout the war. One large contingent led by Colonel Alexander W. Doniphan took a circuitous route, marching, it is claimed, farther than any army since that of Alexander the Great. One of the soldiers who served in Company D of the Missouri Volunteers as William Newcum was really Elizabeth Caroline Newcum. When she became pregnant, she had to leave the service, but several years later, she filed for her veteran's benefits. Since she had witnesses for her time served, a special bill was passed, and she received back pay and some land in Platte County. Missouri militia were also used in Indian territory to assist regular army units in resettling eastern tribes and in campaigns against tribes like the Comanche and Pawnee as westward expansion pushed into more tribes' traditional space. The progressive transition from frontier to farm communities, then to small towns and cities, eluded Missouri. St. Louis was founded in 1763; on the other side of the state, Joplin wasn't settled until 1871. Many communities in the state, especially in the Ozarks, continued to be isolated well into the twentieth century. The fits and starts, the many conflicts and the ever-present threat of violence—both from within and without the community—retarded progress and kept parts of Missouri "wild" far longer than areas in the rest of the state.

Militia service in Missouri was not the same as military service elsewhere. The officers were a mix of aspiring politicians, experienced former military men and natural leaders from frontier communities. The rank and file ran the gamut from veteran fighters to inexperienced farm boys. Many veterans of the War of 1812 had been given bounty land grants in Missouri for their service, adding to the pool of experienced men. In 1820, there were 13 militia regiments and 134 companies totaling 12,030 men. By 1825, there were 31 regiments, but only 8 sent in an annual report. Local militias resisted organizational rules from the state, filling out paperwork and generally being told how to run their business. Muster days were the scene of drunken parties, as officers often provided liquor as an incentive to show up and/or secure votes to keep their positions of leadership. Newspapers produced articles criticizing the practice, observing that it led to "noise, confusion and insubordination" and "bloody noses" after dismissal. Though little formal military training was involved, muster days served a social and political purpose: local leaders would dress in the best uniform they could

Alexander Doniphan. *Courtesy Library of Congress: LC-USZ62-109945.*

put together; veterans of various wars would be honored; and communities would gather as for a fair to watch the drills, hear speeches, conduct business and socialize. Though these militias were not trained to military standards, they were often the only effective fighting forces available on the frontier. There were always plenty of men in these communities who knew how to fight and shoot a gun, and a disproportionate number of them had seen military action.

It is "normal" for different rules of conduct to apply in wartime than in times of peace. Civilized society also has different expectations for a banker in town than for a trapper in the wilderness. The contrasts in lifestyles within the state of Missouri were everywhere to be seen. The river towns were connected by steamboat to the eastern states, while the mining district and trail communities continued to have one foot in the frontier and another in town. Some of the state's better-known residents lived what was seen as half-wild and half-civilized lives. Trappers and explorers like Jim Bridger and William Sublette had homes in Missouri but spent much of their time exploring, trapping, trading and guiding parties through the West. Some had wives and lives in each world, keeping a home and family in St. Louis or Kansas City and having a Native American wife and family on the frontier. Still others were explorers leading parties of surveyors and military forces into Indian territory. These men were the vanguard of what was seen as an invasion by many Native Americans and Mexicans. Though they might have peaceful, even friendly relations with several tribes, they risked their scalps and worse on a regular basis with others. Grizzly bears, panthers and snakes mixed with disease, extreme weather and groups of men who wanted to kill them to make those who survived tough and those who thrived legendary. These men were regularly tapped by the U.S. government and state governments for everything from guiding groups of surveyors, helping negotiators establish treaties with Native American tribes and leading punitive military expeditions. Fur and trading companies employed experienced frontiersmen both to conduct trade negotiations with Native American tribes they had come in contact with and to protect caravans traversing the trails. Men who had shot, stabbed and even scalped their way to prominence were to be counted among the most successful and well-known members of many Missouri communities.

Military service was still a desirable qualification in the West, often used as a stepping-stone to politics. Natural leaders were often called "captain" or "colonel" without regard to any official rank they may have held. Experienced fighters were needed to protect travelers and merchandise, and Missouri always seemed to have a healthy stock of men who had served either in militias or with the regular army. Scouts like Nathan Boone would guide troops, build roads and fortifications, conduct surveys and fight alongside regular army personnel. Their knowledge of the terrain and of the tactics of Native Americans were invaluable both in a fight and in avoiding one. The Spanish floating claims and rights of use had confounded the Americans, with their properly surveyed and titled ideas of property. And the Native Americans' claims to hunting rights or lands they didn't live on year-round was another cause for confusion and conflict. Tribes would vacate lands, only to return for fall or spring hunts. Men who could speak the languages of the various tribes and who understood their history and traditions to some degree were invaluable to both civilian and military employers. Expeditions to the West led by trappers, traders and frontiersmen only increased over time. Whether it was leading hunting expeditions, guiding mapping and planning representatives of the U.S. government or helping mining and railroad engineers push the line of frontier ever westward, there was always work to be had for those with the right skills.

Of the many little wars and almost-wars of the state's first few decades, none would be as devastating as the Border War, which never fully ended but merged with the broader Civil War, which engulfed the entire country. The experiences gained in the little wars created a ready-made set of soldiers to pursue the larger agendas of their leaders, who in many cases had also participated in the little wars. In Missouri, the Civil War came early and stayed late. Born of conflict and created from compromise, the state grew up in a divided family. America was torn apart by its greatest hypocrisy: the land of the free held millions in bondage. Divisions over the expansion of slavery were at play from the country's inception, but a series of political maneuvers in the early 1850s brought the conflict to a boiling point. The Compromise of 1850 put the question of slavery back into the hands of the individual territories applying for statehood. The Fugitive Slave Act (1850) had sparked outrage in the Free States, as officials there were legally bound to assist in the recapture of escaped slaves. The publication of *Uncle Tom's Cabin* in 1852 and increased activity of the Underground Railroad moving escaped slaves out of the United States entirely and into Canada reflected the commitment of the abolitionists and the further polarization of both sides. On Missouri's western border was Indian territory, closed to white settlement. But eastern Kansas had slowly seen squatters and hunting parties from Missouri increase in numbers. The many trails crossing the area, and the push to extend railroad and telegraph lines across the continent, spurred the government to open the territory to settlement.

The Kansas-Nebraska Act set the stage for war in the West, as the war of words in Washington became a call to action for pro- and antislavery forces along the Missouri-Kansas border. Between 1854 and 1861, there was a steadily growing violent conflict between the opposing sides. Immigrant aid societies in many eastern states (not just Massachusetts) were set up to finance groups of Free Staters who would settle in Kansas. Missouri slaveholders feared that a Free State to the west would entice more slaves to run away. They also feared that growth would be shut off for their children who wished to own slaves and large farms. The rush to secure Kansas as a slave state saw thousands of Missourians crossing the border to vote for a proslavery territorial legislature. One leader, Missouri senator David Rice Atchison, had encouraged the group to "kill every god-damned abolitionist in the district if necessary." Atchison had been a major general in the state militia during the Mormon War. General Alexander Doniphan had taken part in three of the little wars. Though he did not lead the ruffians in battle, he funded, gave speeches and encouraged them to move into Kansas. Benjamin Franklin Stringfellow was

Right: David Rice Atchison, a successful politician and leader of the Border Ruffians. *Courtesy Library of Congress: LC-USZ62-109952*.

Below: "The Far West—Shooting Buffalo on the Line of the Kansas Pacific Railroad." *Courtesy Library of Congress: LC-USZ62-133890*.

Two unidentified Border Ruffians with swords. *Courtesy Library of Congress: LC-DIG-ppmsca-40662.*

"The Kansas Row." The cartoon depicts a man resembling Stephen Douglas kicking African Americans out of Kansas and back into Missouri. *Courtesy Library of Congress: LC-USZC6-76.*

a lawyer and a general in the Missouri militia, yet he had no compunction about taking the law into his own hands in dealing with the abolitionists. "I advise one and all to enter every election district in Kansas, in defiance of Reeder and his vile myrmidons, and vote at the point of the bowie-knife and revolver." The proslavery forces took over polls at gunpoint and overwhelmed the Free Staters. The vote was later invalidated due to widespread election fraud (in one county, only 20 of 604 voters were residents of the territory). Newspaper editor Horace Greeley is credited with coining the term *Border Ruffians* to describe the wild men from Missouri who crossed the border and intimidated voters and cast illegal ballots. Kansas territorial governor Andrew Reeder repeated the term in referring to proslavery Weston, Missouri lawyer Benjamin Stringfellow. In response, Stringfellow went to the governor's office and challenged Reeder, knocking him to the ground with a chair and drawing a pistol. Reeder's staff had to restrain Stringfellow to save the governor's life. This was how educated men, community leaders, merchants and lawyers were acting. The run-of-the-mill rowdies were even more willing to wreak havoc.

In 1855, with some funding from fellow abolitionists, John Brown moved to Kansas. His sons were already there, and he was no doubt concerned for his family's well-being as the threat of violence evolved. That same year, 1,200 New England emigrants moved to the territory as part of the organized efforts to seed the state with abolitionist towns. There were proslavery towns like Atchison and Lecompton and Free State towns like Topeka and Manhattan, each peopled largely with recent immigrants. Many of the new arrivals were armed with Sharp's rifles—referred to as Beecher's Bibles (after abolitionist Henry Ward Beecher, who supplied and purchased the guns and the boxes marked "Bibles" they were concealed in). As the conflict widened, violence became commonplace. A group of Border Ruffians (including Daniel Boone's grandson Albert Gallatin Boone) went to the Free State town of Lawrence (named after Emigrant Aid benefactor Amos Lawrence) accompanying Douglas County sheriff Samuel J. Jones with the intention of destroying the two local newspaper offices and the Free State hotel for being "public nuisances." The group of 800 proslavery ruffians destroyed the two presses and threw the type into the river. They then looted the town and tried to destroy the hotel. It took several shots from a cannon, several kegs of gunpowder detonated in the building and, finally, a good torching to do the job, but the men left town with smoldering ruins in their wake. John Brown, hearing of the action in Lawrence, went to work to exact bloody revenge. He and a group including four of his sons went to the homes of supposed proslavery Kansans near

John Brown. *Courtesy Library of Congress: LC-USZ62-137591.*

Pottawatomie and took five men out of their homes and hacked them to death with broadswords. Brown was involved in more violent encounters in Kansas, but eventually he left the state and attacked the federal arsenal at Harpers Ferry with the hope of arming and leading a slave revolt. He was captured and hanged, but there were dozens of fanatical abolitionists in Kansas to take his place. To many, he was a martyr for the abolitionist cause.

The future status of Kansas in terms of slavery was far from the only motivating force behind the Border War. There were fanatics and idealists on both sides of the line, but there were also many who saw merely an opportunity. Looting as punishment became a career on both

Henry Ward Beecher. *Courtesy Library of Congress: C-DIG-cwpbh-03065.*

James Henry Lane. *Courtesy Library of Congress: LC-DIG-ppmsca-11516.*

sides of the Missouri-Kansas border in the 1850s. Farms and villages, even whole towns, were open for the taking, and both sides took. Initially, the Missouri raiders came into Kansas and stole in order to "punish" the easterners for trying to take over land far from their homes instead of allowing the normal progression of settlement from nearby states. The Kansas raiders ("Jayhawkers" and "Red Legs" led by men like Senator James Lane and Colonel Charles Jennison) started out with forays to liberate slaves but devolved into carrying out punitive attacks and large-scale destruction of property and outright theft. On the Missouri side of the border, there had been settlement for more than thirty years, and there were fine farms and homes to loot and lots of livestock to steal. Wealthy families who had built up businesses and homes on the trail trade often owned slaves and became targets as much for their property as for their sympathies. Likewise, Kansas had new communities freshly provisioned by aid societies—tempting targets for "ruffians" justifying theft under the guise of politics or revenge. The communities on the Kansas side of the border had a tenuous hold at best in the mid-1850s, but as help poured in from the East, men and arms sufficient to solidify their position fell into place. Missourians would continue to do damage in Kansas for years, but the nature of warfare on the border would become more desperate. Though few Missourians had participated in the Border War, the northern press painted the worst possible picture of the state, and the southern press praised its residents just as loudly. The net effect was to create a negative stereotype that many would apply to Missourians regardless of their position on secession, slavery or states' rights. The drums of war that had sounded the alarm up and down the border between Kansas and Missouri were heard in the East, the South and the North. With the advent of civil war, many of the Kansas militias were incorporated into regular army units or worked under the legitimizing auspices of the U.S. Army. The little war between Kansas and Missouri became part of the bigger war, and Kansas achieved statehood as a Free State in 1860, on the eve of that great conflict.

4

RUFFIANS, BUSHWHACKERS AND GUERRILLAS

In the 1860 presidential election, Abraham Lincoln got about 10 percent of the vote in Missouri, but Missouri was not a secessionist state. Both Democratic Party and Constitutional Union Party representatives garnered the majority of support. Neither Stephen Douglas (D) nor John Bell (CU) supported secession during the campaign, and even though Bell owned slaves, he had opposed expansion of slavery into the West. Douglas, who ultimately received Missouri's nine electoral votes, had tried to skirt the moral issue and blindly argued that slavery was a matter best left to the voters of each territory or state. The experiment in popular sovereignty that turned into the horrific Border War in Kansas had proven his argument impractical but had not deterred his support of democracy over morality. To many people, he thus ceded the high ground to Lincoln. In the governor's race, Claiborne Jackson had supported Douglas out of political expediency, but unlike the majority of Missourians, he was willing to support the South even in secession. He began showing his true colors in his inaugural speech: "The first drop of blood shed in a war of aggression upon a sovereign state will arouse a spirit which must result in the overthrow of our entire Federal system, and which this generation will never see quelled....The destiny of the slave-holding states of this union is one and the same. So long as a state continues to maintain slavery within her limits, it is impossible to separate her fate from that of her sister states." It was a matter of weeks before the state was divided into two armed camps. Within a few months, the popularly elected government and its head would be driven from the state by a Federal army.

Missouri, like Kentucky and other Border States, was caught in a quandary. A significant portion of its population had ties to the South, and there were many communities whose livelihood was tied to the slave economy. In towns like Lexington, Boonville and Independence, leading citizens, bankers and large-scale farmers had thousands of dollars invested in slaves. It was one thing to stop expansion in Kansas, quite another to ask these men to join an army that would invade states where they had families and to give up "property" worth thousands (millions in today's dollars) without compensation. The owner of the largest number of slaves in Missouri was Jabez Smith of Jackson County. Smith (originally from Virginia) not only used slaves to work his own property; he also raised and sold them like livestock and rented them out as skilled workers to smaller farmers and businessmen in the community. His books had loans and rental agreements with dozens of small farmers in the county. He and other community leaders faced economic crises, which meant that everyone they did business with also feared ruin. It was not just the wealthy slave owner in Missouri who felt threatened economically by abolition, but also entire communities. When Missourians were forced to take sides, thousands were moved by kinship and personal ties or economic self-interest to support the South. Frank James joined the Missouri State Guard, as did Cole Younger. The sons of men who had settled the frontier, built successful farms and businesses and served their country in war and in peace in various social and political positions went off to war—to fight for democracy or for states' rights; to keep the slaves they had or to keep their neighbors from losing theirs; to fight against northern aggression; or just to fight. After all, they had been raised to do so.

Missouri was not a secessionist state. Its governor, Claiborne Jackson, ran as an anti-secession Douglas Democrat, but after the election, his true intentions became known. Jackson called a special state convention to consider the question of secession (which he lobbied in favor of). The convention voted 98–1 against. Jackson claimed he intended to continue the policy of armed neutrality, but he called up the state militias on the pretense that they were preparing to defend against a Confederate invasion. In April 1861, President Lincoln called for the states to provide militias for the federal government to use in response to the attack on Fort Sumter.

Each governor was sent a letter with a quota of militiamen he was expected to provide. Jackson's response is legendary: "Your requisition is illegal, unconstitutional, revolutionary, inhuman, diabolical and cannot and will not be complied with." Meanwhile, Jackson was in communication with Jefferson Davis, asking for cannon to use to take over the Federal arsenal at St. Louis. He appointed Sterling Price to lead the militia. Price had been a state representative, a U.S. congressman, a brigadier general in the Mexican-American War and the eleventh governor of Missouri.

The commander of the Federal arsenal at St. Louis was Captain Nathaniel Lyon, an ardent abolitionist and absolute supporter of union. Lyon correctly anticipated the governor's intentions and used Federal troops and members of a pro-Union paramilitary group to surround Camp Jackson outside of St. Louis. The militiamen were disarmed and marched through the street. The mob in St. Louis included many sympathetic southerners, some of whom threw rocks and debris at Lyon's men. Apparently, a drunken member of the crowd stumbled in front of the soldiers and, accidently or not, fired a gun. The soldiers shot into the crowd, killing twenty-eight and wounding dozens more. In the chaos that followed, two Federals and three militiamen were killed and others were wounded. After the initial shock, there were riots for the next few days, until Federal troops enforced martial law. Price and Jackson appealed to General William S. Harney (commander of the Department of the West and Lyon's superior) to make a truce. The resulting Price-Harney Truce left Federal forces in charge of St. Louis and the Missouri State Guard in charge of protecting the rest of the state. Jackson convinced the legislature to pass a bill giving him broad executive powers and placing Major General Sterling Price at the head of the militia (which included all men of age in the state). If accepted, these acts would have had the same effect as secession.

In St. Louis, politician Frank Blair had been a major player both for preserving union and pressing the Republican agenda. Using his connections in Washington, he was able to get Harney replaced with the freshly promoted Brigadier General Lyon. In June 1861, Blair and Lyon met with Jackson and Price at the Planter's House Hotel in St. Louis. Jackson wanted to extend the earlier arrangement that had forced the Federal authority to limit itself to the St. Louis area and left the state guard under his direction controlling the rest of the state. Lyon was aghast at his position and at one point rose and said, "Rather than concede to the State of Missouri for one single instant the right to dictate to my Government in any manner, however unimportant I will see you, and you, and you [pointing to each of the participants] and every man woman and child in the State of Missouri dead and buried. This means war!" Price and Jackson were escorted out and allowed to leave by train, but they stopped and tore up some of the tracks behind them for fear of pursuit. Lyon gathered troops and headed for Jefferson City by steamboat, but by the time he arrived, the governor and state guard had moved to Boonville. Lyon moved quickly to secure the railroads, the ferry crossings and the rivers. Price and Jackson were forced to the southwest corner of the state.

In Jefferson City, the Missouri State Convention reconvened and, on July 23, 1861, declared the office of governor and several others vacant. Former Missouri chief justice Hamilton Gamble was appointed governor, and a pro-Union provisional state government was appointed to replace the legislators who had fled. An oath of allegiance to the provisional as well as federal government was required to hold office in the state. Missouri ceased to be a democracy for the remainder of the war. Jackson refused to accept the authority of the appointed government and would eventually gather some of the elected legislators at Neosho to declare secession in October. Lyon was killed in August at the Battle of Wilson's Creek, and in November, the Confederacy recognized Missouri as its twelfth state. The problem was that Missouri was not a secessionist state, the Federal army controlled the rails and rivers and Price and Jackson could not take or hold the state. It seemed that Missouri was a rebel state in name only, but that would soon change.

Shortly before General Lyon's death, John Frémont was placed in charge of the Department of the West. Lyon had requested reinforcements, but Frémont focused on protecting Cairo, Illinois, and traffic on the Mississippi River, sending troops and a new commander there (Brigadier General Ulysses S. Grant). Capitalizing on his victory at Wilson's Creek, Price had moved up the Kansas line, and then turned east to attack Union forces at Lexington, Missouri. Price hoped to regain control of the river so that recruits could cross and come south to join his forces. Price's numbers were increasing at that time and successfully overwhelmed the smaller Union force stationed at Lexington. Frémont had gathered 25,000 men at St. Louis but failed to send reinforcements in a timely manner to Lexington. When he did move, he had nearly 40,000 men. Marching toward Sedalia, he threatened Price's ability to rejoin Confederate forces in Arkansas. Unable to feed and arm the large number of recruits he had gathered at Lexington, Price had to retreat south and leave most of his recent volunteers behind. Frémont took a number of missteps in his short tenure leading the Department of the West. In response to Price's use of guerrilla forces in Missouri (to disrupt rail traffic and make breaks in the Federal lines for recruits to come south and join

Major General Sterling Price. *Courtesy Library of Congress: LC-DIG-cwpb-07527.*

his command), Frémont made an emancipation proclamation that included the slaves of anyone caught in arms against the Federal government and anyone who aided them. Wealthy planters who had hoped to sit out the war in neutral Missouri were driven into the fray, as were their sons and many they did business with. Lincoln tried to get Frémont to withdraw the order voluntarily; failing that, Lincoln replaced him with General Henry Halleck and allowed Hamilton Gamble to ease martial law and remove Frémont's emancipation rule.

In his brief tenure, Frémont had appointed General John Pope commander of the District of North Missouri and later the District of Central Missouri. Guerrilla activity in the state was widespread, and Pope held whole communities financially accountable for the actions of these small groups. In August 1861, J.T.K. Howard (general agent of the Hannibal and St. Joseph Railroad) wrote to Frémont and, through an intermediary, to Secretary of War Edwin Stanton, complaining of Union troops shooting civilians from trains for sport, looting homes, raping slaves and stealing horses. Local officers would send men into homes to gather "payment" for damage done by guerrillas and basically loot them at gunpoint. This heavy-handed approach sent Rebels flocking to the guerrilla ranks. Pope's men were mostly from northern states, and his officers did little to check their actions in dealing with the civilian population. In 1861, the North Missouri Railroad reported that more than one hundred miles of railroad tracks had been demolished, nearly every bridge had been set on fire and thirty cars and one engine had been destroyed by guerrillas.

In December, General Halleck put out General Orders No. 32, which expanded use of the death penalty for burning bridges and destroying railroads and telegraph lines. Anyone caught in the act could be shot on sight or, if accused, could be arrested, tried by military commission and, if found guilty, executed. By January 1862, Halleck had again expanded the death penalty to include anyone, including Missouri State Guard units, involved in guerrilla activity. Only uniformed Confederate soldiers from seceded states were to be afforded prisoner-of-war status. The Black Flag (signifying no quarter) was hoisted by both sides. Guerrillas started executing captured soldiers. Halleck eventually promoted Pope to command the Department of the Mississippi, but the damage in the north was done. In northwest Missouri, guerrilla Silas M. Gordon met with similar help from Union commander David Hunter. Gordon had kidnapped Union officers, briefly taken over the town of Weston and was believed to have derailed a train near St. Joseph. He and thirty to forty of his men were camped out in Platte City, Missouri, when Commander Hunter sent word from Fort Leavenworth that Gordon was to be handed over. If not, the town was to be burned. The locals could not have captured or delivered Gordon even if they particularly wanted to. Troops were sent out, the town was burned and Gordon's ranks swelled. The pattern of punishing ordinary Missourians for the actions of guerrillas would be repeated throughout the war, with escalating consequences for both sides. Halleck couldn't keep the railroads running—it was too easy to burn a bridge or tear up some track—and it only took a few guerrillas to tie up thousands of troops trying to protect train traffic. Attempts to capture Gordon by burning Platte City failed—twice. Gordon survived the war, moved to Texas and ran a trading post at Gordonville, a small town that is named for him.

Along the western border, things got worse. In July 1861, Colonel Van Horn sent Colonel Charles Jennison and his men to Harrisonville to check a rumor that Confederate troops were forming there. Though Jennison found no troops, he still looted the stores, including Henry Younger's livery stable. Younger was pro-Union, but they took $4,000 in carriages and wagons and forty saddle horses from him just the same. In August, Senator James H. Lane led troops from Kansas in an attempt to turn Price back south after Wilson's Creek. At the Battle of Dry Wood Creek, Lane was forced back to Fort Scott, and Price captured a number of the Kansans' mules and then continued on to Lexington. Lane went back down the border, not to attack Price but to punish all the towns that he felt supported the Missourians. In September 1861, Lane entered Osceola, Missouri, a town with a population of more than two thousand people. Some of his men found a small cache of arms, and Lane used it to condemn the whole community. His men burned all but three buildings in the town. Osceola had been home to Union soldiers and supporters, but Lane's men made few distinctions. A drumhead court led to the execution of nine citizens. Lane left Osceola with 300 wagonloads of loot (and several drunken soldiers), 350 horses and mules and 200 Negroes, tallying $1,000,000 in stolen or destroyed property for the trip. The goods went to Lawrence to be divided and distributed to the raiders while Price's army was far away. In December, Jennison moved into Jackson County, Missouri, robbing and looting homes, farms and citizens regardless of which side they supported (once again looting homes of Union soldiers). Jennison's men killed one man in Independence for refusing to give them liquor and another for trying to save his mules from them by swimming them across the river. By December 1861, Halleck wrote General George McClellan: "The conduct of the forces under Lane and Jennison has done more for the enemy in this State than could have been accomplished by 20,000 of his own army....It is rumored that Lane has been made a brigadier-general. I cannot conceive of a more injudicious appointment. It will take 20,000 men to counteract its effect in this State, and, moreover, is offering a premium for rascality and robbing generally." Finally, in January 1862, he ordered General Pope to drive Lane and Jennison out of the state, but once again it was too little, too late, and the guerrilla ranks would swell once again as spring weather warmed the woods.

Nobody knew who would win the war, especially in Missouri in 1861. Union forces had lost at the First Battle of Bull Run, and Price had won at Wilson's Creek and Lexington. Guerrillas were doing damage all over the state, and Federal forces were unable to stop them. Some of the guerrilla groups were organized and led by Price's officers, but others were formed around local leaders with no direct chain of command. Missouri's most notorious guerrilla wasn't even from Missouri. William Quantrill was born in Ohio in 1837 and received sufficient education there by age sixteen to begin work as a teacher. Though he found occasional employment in that

Jemison's (sic) Jayhawkers, by Aldabert Volck. Jennison's Jayhawkers were as notorious for pillage and murder in Missouri as Quantrill was in Kansas. *Courtesy Library of Congress: LC-USZ62-100061.*

field, Quantrill ended up working a number of other jobs just to get by. In 1858, he was in the Kansas Territory, a failed farmer who, according to his letters, supported Lane and the antislavery men. The next year, he was with a group of Border Ruffians capturing slaves for bounty. At the start of 1860, he was back in Lawrence teaching school. By the end of 1860, he had led a group of Kansas raiders on a slave-freeing expedition, only to slip ahead as a "scout" and warn slave owners of the raid and join them in attacking the Kansans. He excused his actions with a fabrication that was told far and wide of how he was originally from Maryland, and while in Kansas, he and a brother were ambushed by abolitionist raiders of James Montgomery. He claimed that his brother was killed and that he was wounded. His part in the raid was payback, he claimed. The bogus story was believed, and he became a sort of local hero.

By the spring of 1861, Quantrill had moved down into the Cherokee Nation and befriended Joel Mayes, a war chief. He joined Mayes's group under Brigadier General Benjamin McCullough during the Battle of Wilson's Creek and then joined Price's forces at the Battle of Lexington. It was claimed that he learned guerrilla tactics from Mayes, but it was a short tutelage, as Quantrill was with him just a few months. Quantrill left Price's force and started his own guerrilla band in November 1861. Starting with around a dozen young men, Quantrill began ambushing Jennison's and Montgomery's patrols, stealing back slaves and livestock from the Kansans and causing alarm among the Federal troops, who never knew where the next attack was coming from. By February 1862, Captain W.S. Oliver wrote to General Pope that, in the vicinity of Blue Springs, Quantrill and his gang had robbed mails and stole the coaches and horses. Being mounted on the best horses in the country, the gang members defied pursuit. Quantrill and his group were pursued by Federal and militia forces that far outnumbered them. He and his men knew that capture likely meant death. In *Gray Ghosts of the Confederacy*, Richard S. Brownlee explains that "Quantrill's service eliminated all but the wildest rider, the best pistol shot, the boy with the least regard for personal safety." In January, Jennison's men burned Dayton and Columbus, and in March, Quantrill retaliated by looting Aubry, Kansas, burning one house and riding right through Union patrols back to Missouri. Quantrill raided a recruiting post in Liberty in March 1862 while Union troops were looking for him to the south in Jackson County. When troops were sent to Clay County to find him, he moved back to Jackson and burned the Blue River Bridge on the road from Independence to Kansas City.

All through the spring of 1862, as Federal armies began winning battles, Missouri's guerrilla forces were growing larger and their attacks were becoming more effective. By summer, Colonel James T. Buel said he'd lost so many troops protecting mail that he would no longer send it. Instead, he began forcing secessionists to carry it. In June and July, Quantrill's group ambushed the Little Blue River ferry; attacked mail escorts and patrols in Cass, Johnson and Jackson Counties; and captured a steamboat, *Little Blue*, loaded with military supplies, at Sibley. Quantrill and his men had a number of narrow escapes that year, and he made several costly mistakes: he was caught with his entire command on the David Tate farm, but they managed to fight their way out, losing several men in the process. He attacked the Union post at Warrensburg that was fortified with a thick board stockade around the brick courthouse and had to leave nine dead and carry away seventeen wounded for his trouble. With each narrow escape, his core group of survivors was learning the deadly skills they would pass on to the next batch of recruits. Quantrill's men maximized firepower, with each carrying several .36-caliber Colt revolvers instead of the less accurate .44-caliber gun and mixing carbines for distance and shotguns for closer fighting. Gathering information under disguise, coordinating attacks, feigning weakness or retreat in order to draw enemy troops into an ambush, having pre-planned routes of dispersal and even setting up relays of fresh horses all became part of the guerrillas' methodology.

In July 1862, the Confederacy passed the Partisan Ranger Act, and Major General Thomas C. Hindman quickly put it into play in Missouri. Hindman had already taken steps to secure Arkansas as a base from which to do damage to Federal troops in Missouri and up the Mississippi River. He chose officers, including the following: Colonel Upton Hayes (a descendant of Daniel Boone), Colonel Joseph C. Porter, Colonel John T. Hughes

William Quantrill. *Courtesy Wikimedia Commons.*

(Mexican-American War veteran, state representative and cousin to Sterling Price), Colonel J. Vard Cockrell (of Warrensburg; his father was sheriff there), Colonel John T. Coffee (politician, Speaker of the Missouri House of Representatives), Colonel Gideon W. Thompson, Colonel Warner Lewis, Colonel J.A. Poindexter and Captain Joseph O. Shelby. These men were sent out to various parts of Missouri to organize and recruit bands of guerrillas. General John Schofield made the claim that these officers had enrolled from 30,000 to 50,000 men in Missouri; the actual number was likely less than 10 percent of the exaggerated estimate. William Quantrill was promoted to captain by M. Jeff Thompson in August 1862. Captain Quantrill would use his position to legitimize his excesses, just as Lane and Jennison had done.

In July 1862, Brigadier General John Schofield put out General Orders No. 19, requiring universal military service in the state, and sent troops into the homes of thousands of residents on the pretext of searching for weapons or supplies for the guerrillas. In August, Order No. 9 allowed that, while pursuing guerrillas, Union soldiers were given authority to obtain necessary supplies from guerrillas and those who supported them. This led to pillaging by militiamen all over the state. Even though guerrillas were being captured and killed, there were plenty of recruits to replenish their ranks. In northeast Missouri, Colonel Joseph Porter gathered more than 300 men but broke from hit-and-run tactics. As a result, he stalled trying to take on the Federals in direct engagements. Quantrill continued to use the tactic, as well as surprise attacks and traps. On August 11, he attacked Independence at 4:30 a.m. with 350 horse-riding Rebels screaming down the streets, shooting and shouting. The Union forces there were split; of the 300 stationed there, 37 were killed, 63 were wounded, 150 were captured and the rest retreated to Kansas City. By September, another leadership change was made. Schofield was removed by Major General Samuel R. Curtis. It was estimated that during the first few years of the war, more than 60,000 troops had been tied up in Missouri fighting no more than 3,000 or 4,000 guerrillas. In March, the Confederates had lost the Battle of Pea Ridge. They were pushed farther back at Cane Hill and Prairie Grove. Union forces had taken New Madrid, then Island No. 10. Corinth and New Orleans soon followed. The war in the West was becoming isolated from the war in the East. The guerrillas in Missouri had to wage their own war against an enemy that could and would chase them from their homes, confiscate all they owned and shoot them without trial.

In the winter of 1862–63, Quantrill joined Confederate forces in Arkansas. In May 1863, they were back in Missouri, and Union troops were once again searching for them. A patrol in search of Frank James arrived on the family farm and began to torture the James brothers' stepfather, Dr. Reuben Samuel, by hanging him briefly. Fifteen-year-old Jesse supposedly tried to stop them and was beaten with a whip. Samuels sustained permanent damage from the hanging, and Jesse joined the guerrillas. By August 1863, the guerrillas' return had led to the onerous Order No. 10, which gave Federal troops the task of arresting and removing from the state of Missouri the relatives of known guerrillas, including wives, sisters and mothers. One group of women and girls held under the order was imprisoned in a building in Kansas City owned by painter George Caleb Bingham. By fair or foul cause, the building collapsed, wounding and killing several of the prisoners. Among the killed and injured were two cousins of the Younger brothers and two sisters of Bill Anderson (one of whom was killed, the other crippled). Within a week of the collapse, the various guerrilla leaders had gathered a force of more than 300 men and set out for Lawrence, Kansas. Bent on revenge, desirous of loot and armed to the teeth, they rode boldly past Union posts on the border. They arrived on August 21 at 5:00 a.m., took over the Eldridge Hotel (a brick building at the highest point in town) and then fanned out to begin killing, burning and looting. They robbed the banks and businesses as well as private citizens. By the end of the day, more than 150 men and boys of the town had been killed and a quarter of the buildings, including all but two businesses,

M. Jeff Thompson. *Courtesy Wikimedia Commons.*

had been looted and burned. Added to the human toll was $2 million in damage to property, including the destruction of three newspaper offices. Quantrill had instructed his men not to harm any women, but unarmed men and teenage boys were fair game—after all, Quantrill's "men" were mostly teens and men in their twenties themselves. Quantrill had just turned twenty-six the month before; his lieutenants, Dave Poole and John Thrailkill, were slightly younger; and William Anderson was only twenty-three and his lieutenant, Archie Clement, only seventeen.

In response to the Lawrence attack, General Thomas Ewing drafted Order No. 11, which forced the evacuation of rural areas of four counties in Missouri. To make matters worse, Jennison's men and other Kansas troops were sent in to enforce the order. They burned houses, looted businesses and killed residents. In Cass County, 600 people remained from a prewar population of 10,000. Even fewer remained in Bates County. Far from stopping the guerrillas, Ewing only enraged them further. Quantrill began to take a back seat to his lieutenants. Bill Anderson, who had merely been one of Quantrill's allies before Lawrence, became known as "Bloody" Bill Anderson. He quite possibly lost his tenuous grip on sanity after the death and crippling of his sisters. In July 1864, Anderson robbed the bank at Huntsville (a town he had lived in as a child) with around 100 men. His

The Lawrence Massacre. *Courtesy Library of Congress: LC-USZ62-134452.*

command's attacks on Federal troops included killing the men, stripping the bodies (clothing, especially coats and shoes, were a prime commodity), sometimes scalping the dead and then leaving cryptic notes on the bodies to inspire fear in those who found them. They burned bridges, robbed whole towns, attacked riverboats and ferries, drank the town's saloons dry and looted pro-Union stores. In late August, they took over a tugboat, killed the captain and took the craft for a drunken joyride up and down the river. In September 1864, they robbed a train of four carloads of Union cavalry horses. Incredibly difficult to track, the gang would be spotted in one town and then show up forty miles away the next day after riding all night. Also that month, Anderson robbed thirteen stages, stopped steamboat traffic in central Missouri and, with groups led by George Todd and John Thrailkill, wiped out a twelve-wagon military train near Rocheport. The gang made off with 18,000 rounds of ammunition, a wagonload of uniforms and 1,000 rations.

On September 27, 1862, Bloody Bill entered Centralia with a group of 30 men, hoping to find a St. Louis paper or some other news on General Sterling Price's return/invasion of Missouri. They started off looting the town and robbing the stage as it pulled in. A train from St. Charles then arrived to find blocked tracks. Onboard were 125 passengers, including 23 unarmed Union soldiers on leave. The soldiers were pulled aside, told to strip and were then executed and mutilated. The depot was set on fire. The train was set ablaze and sent, with the whistle tied down and blowing, down the track toward Sturgeon. A mounted Union patrol of 147 men rode into Centralia around 3:30 that afternoon and determined to chase down the guerrillas. Anderson had rejoined the rest of his men by that time. When the Federal force came upon the guerrillas, the commander ordered them to dismount and fire. After the first volley, Anderson's mounted Rebels rode at full gallop toward the Federals before they could reload and mowed them down. In the shootout, 123 Union soldiers were killed. They, too, were stripped and mutilated in a carnival of blood.

With a leader driven to the brink of madness and bent on revenge or death—and their own lives daily at stake—the young men in Anderson's charge had witnessed so much callousness and cruelty that no act upon the enemy was considered too depraved. On October 3, guerrillas robbed and burned two trains on the Hannibal St. Jo line at Hunnewell. With Price at the head of an army of more than 12,000 troops entering the state and the guerrillas doing damage everywhere, the Hannibal and St. Jo suspended train traffic west of St. Charles. In mid-October, George Todd stopped the

Pacific Railroad line at Otterville by burning the bridge, depot and water tanks there. The guerrillas seemed to have things well in hand in advance of Price's invasion. But Price failed to take St. Louis, avoided Jefferson City and was defeated at Westport. His army was devastated as a fighting force at Mine Creek.

Missouri was not a secessionist state. Nearly three times as many Missourians served in the Union army and in the Missouri State Militia as in the Confederacy, state guard and guerrilla groups. Going into the winter of 1864–65, it was becoming clear that the cause was lost. Guerrilla leader George Todd was killed at the Second Battle of Independence. Bloody Bill was drawn into an ambush and killed in late October. His body was dragged through the street of nearby Richmond, photographed and then a finger was cut off to get the ring attached to it. His head was cut off and put on a telegraph pole. His body was later buried in the local cemetery, and a week later, a group of Jennison's men came through and was incensed at seeing that locals had piled flowers on the grave. It is claimed that they kicked the flowers off and relieved themselves on the spot. The following

Martial Law, George Caleb Bingham painting decrying Order No. 11. *Courtesy Library of Congress: LC-DIG-pga-02633.*

Thomas Ewing, infamous for Order No. 11 evicting the population of four Missouri counties. *Courtesy Library of Congress: LC-DIG-cwpb-06175.*

summer, William Quantrill and a small group of guerrillas were ambushed in Kentucky. Quantrill was shot and became paralyzed from the chest down. He died a few days later, on June 6, 1865, at age twenty-seven.

BRICK BULLPENS

By midcentury, many Missouri towns were beyond the frontier stage, with second- and third-generation families investing in homes and businesses often made of brick. City and county offices on the town square were being built with more thought of the impression they would make on visitors. In 1859, Jackson County built a two-story brick home and office for the county marshal at 217 North Main Street in Independence. From the street, its outward appearance was not significantly different from the other buildings and businesses lining the square. The home was built in the Federal style, and the offices had a separate entrance on the north side of the building facing the street. Out of sight, built onto the back of the marshal's office and home, was the two-story jail with thick limestone walls and a dozen cells, each with a double set of heavy steel doors. The nice home and office facing Main Street with the stone walls and iron bars concealed either behind or within was a style repeated across the state, from Hannibal (1878) to Nevada (1860). In this combination jail and marshal's office and home, prisoners could be processed, locked up and held while awaiting trial. The county marshal could attend to the needs of the court more readily and be

1859 Marshal's Home & Jail, Independence, Missouri. *Author's collection.*

Cooper County Sheriff's Office & Jail at Boonville. *Author's collection.*

available to the citizenry from a central location. Pressures from growth and expansion coupled with the Border War and Civil War may have sparked the construction of new and larger jails in Independence and Nevada. Whether or not they were anticipating a spike in prisoners, the jails built in towns along the border had plenty of business in the 1850s and '60s.

Remaining nineteenth-century brick jails include the 1855 jail in Mount Vernon (the second county jail); the 1878 jail in Hannibal; and jails in Pilot Grove (1892), Linnaeus (1871), Potosi (1893) and Gallatin (1889). In Boonville, the sheriff's office and jail is split down the middle, brick on one side and stone on the other (with a hanging barn out back). Doubtless, there are others still standing; a complete list is a work in progress. I have traced former city- and county-owned jails through multiple uses. Some have been sold for private use or repurposed as offices, firehouses or garages. In 2005, both the Howard County and the Randolph County jails were sold on eBay. The sale of the Howard County jail in Fayette convinced Randolph County officials to follow suit and offer up the old jail in Huntsville. In the twentieth century, a combination of factors led to the destruction of many brick buildings in the central or downtown districts of many cities and towns across the state. Sometimes, it was just a case of being cheaper to start from scratch than to upgrade and update the old buildings to emerging standards. Some of the remaining buildings are in a sort of limbo while local communities try to decide whether to preserve, repurpose or dispose of them.

5

THE UNDEFEATED

fter nearly two years of living on the run, always outnumbered, a death sentence hanging over his head, it was coming to an end. Bloody Bill was dead, Quantrill was dead and Lee and the Confederacy had folded. Seventeen-year-old Jesse James was considering his options. He was born in September 1847, joined Bill Anderson's guerrillas when he was around sixteen and took part in the carnival of blood and destruction that followed in their wake. It was May 1865 when the eighteen-year-old veteran approached Union troops in Lexington, Missouri. He later claimed he intended to surrender. It didn't work out. Before he could get close, the Federals put a bullet through Jesse's lung and changed the world. Had he surrendered, signed his oath of allegiance and reentered society, Jesse James may well have ended his days as a relatively unknown farmer in northwest Missouri. Instead, after recovering from his wound, he rejoined Archie Clement's band of outlaws and continued attacking soft targets as if the war had never ended.

Over time, Jesse James would become the best known of the Missouri guerrillas who either could not or would not surrender. Older brother Frank had stayed with Quantrill to the end then gained his parole in Kentucky in 1865 and returned to the family farm. The victorious North had little sympathy or patience for these men. In Missouri, those who had supported the South were disenfranchised, and the Radical Republicans had enacted laws that made it nearly impossible for former Rebels to participate in civil society. Oaths of allegiance were required—even of ministers—to serve in any public capacity and often included wording that excluded anyone who had opposed the Union in the past. Guerrillas who had kept a step ahead of the more numerous Federal troops for years, as well as military units that had won many battles in the state, weren't ready to capitulate just because Robert E. Lee had given up. General Jo Shelby gathered his forces and headed south, stopping at the Rio Grande to bury the flag he and his Missourians would not surrender in battle. Shelby and roughly one thousand of his men traveled on to Mexico to offer their services to Emperor Maximilian rather than accept defeat. Ex-guerrilla John Thrailkill went to Mexico with Price and Shelby and ended up being successful in the mining, railroad and cattle businesses. He died in Mexico City in 1895. Jesse James couldn't bring himself to permanently leave his home, family and friends in Missouri, so he remained. There were still hundreds of ex-guerrillas and former confederate militiamen living in the state.

Open warfare between large troop concentrations had ended. But there were still groups of armed young men, experienced fighters who felt they had no normal life to return to. Several of Bloody Bill's men, under the leadership of Archie Clement, began a new career, starting at the Clay County Savings and Loan in Liberty, Missouri, in February 1866. Though concrete proof of who was or wasn't involved is lacking, witnesses identified five members of the gang as former guerrillas: Oliver Shepherd, Bud and Donnie Pence, Frank Gregg and Jim Wilkinson. Robbing banks and harassing Republicans was an easy transition for the boys. Though Frank and Jesse were suspects in a number of robberies that they may or may not have been involved in, they, too, eventually followed in Clement's footsteps and began a career that would lead to fame, a little fortune and, for Jesse, an early death at age thirty-four.

On October 30, the Alexander Mitchell Bank at Lexington was robbed by four unidentified men. They were pursued by a posse led by former guerrilla Dave Poole and three other ex-guerrillas who were likely in on the heist themselves. Needless to say, the posse made no arrests. On May 22, 1867, the Hughes and Wasson Bank in Richmond, Missouri, was robbed by a dozen or more gunmen. Three townspeople were killed, and warrants were made out for nine men, six of whom were former guerrillas: Dick Burns, Payne Jones, Ike Flannery, Andy McGuire, Tom Little and Allen Parmer (a brother-in-law of Frank and Jesse James). Little and McGuire were arrested but never made it to trial, as they were lynched by mobs at Richmond and Warrensburg, respectively. In March 1868, ex-guerrilla George Shepherd was arrested for robbing the bank at Russellville, Kentucky. The James

Jesse James as a young man with gun. *Courtesy Library of Congress: LC-USZ62-3855.*

brothers were accused of robbing the bank at Gallatin in December 1869. By failing to turn themselves in for trial (and possible lynching, as with Little and McGuire), they were officially dubbed outlaws. Cole Younger and Clell Miller were accused of robbing a train at Otterville in 1876. The list went on and on. Missouri had become the "Outlaw State," and while the pain and suffering of Reconstruction, a Radical Republican government and a divided and broken populace made few headlines, the daring and desperate acts of a few of its young men would soon be known around the world.

It has been estimated that all the Missouri guerrilla groups together amounted to between two and three thousand fighters, and the Kansas "Jayhawkers" and "Red Legs" might have included a few hundred men. Even with those small numbers, after the war, the majority of these men returned to legitimate civilian occupations. Some communities were more accepting than others, and therein lay the problem. Where bitterness and desire for revenge ruled, communities were divided. Where there was a strong Federal troop presence, ex-Confederates felt a boot on their homeland. Where the ex-Rebels were the majority, outsiders and Union supporters were treated like the enemy. Several thousand Federal troops were sent back into Missouri in 1866. In an attempt to deal with lawlessness, the state had ordered all men over eighteen to register in case they were needed for service in the Missouri State Militia or face a twenty-dollar fine. Archie Clement contacted the military authorities at Lexington and offered to come in and register if they would let him.

On December 13, 1866, Clement rode into Lexington at the head of a column of twenty-six men, all armed to the teeth. They went to the City Hotel and had dinner and a few drinks. They then walked to the militia office in the courthouse and registered and left town (they were encouraged to leave once their civic duty was done). The tense situation was resolved, but Clement decided to go back to the hotel bar and keep drinking. The militia's major, knowing that disobedience would lead to trouble, sent three men to arrest Clement, but he shot his way out and mounted a horse to ride out of town. As he passed the courthouse, he was shot at from several windows and fell dead in the street. Archie Clement was dead at age twenty, but the gang lived on. Young men who had committed countless crimes of pillaging, looting and killing during the war felt little desire to settle back down to tending farms. For these young men, the adrenaline rush of riding into town hollering with guns blazing and riding out loaded down with money and other loot far exceeded the simple pleasure of slopping the hogs.

One of Quantrill's ex-guerrillas was James "Jim Crow" Chiles, a member of a prominent pro-southern Jackson County family. His father was a two-time state senator. Chiles was married to Sarah Ann Young, the sister of Martha Ellen Young-Truman, making him the uncle of President Harry Truman. After the war, Chiles had trouble adjusting to the new order. The Ironclad Oath under Missouri's Drake Constitution required one to be

Arch Clement. *Courtesy Missouri Valley Special Collections, Kansas City Public Library, Kansas City, Missouri.*

"innocent" of eighty-six separate actions or stated beliefs in order to hold public office, vote, serve as an officer in a private corporation or even work for a railroad. Anyone who had even publicly expressed sympathy for the Confederate cause was considered a traitor and unfit for any of a number of positions or even to vote. Chiles was well known for his beliefs and the violent life he had lived during the war. He ran a gaming house and saloon in Kansas City and had been accused of killing nine men after the war and was under indictment for the deaths of three men when he got into a confrontation with Jackson County marshal James Peacock. In September 1873, Jim Chiles crossed paths with Marshal Peacock on Liberty Street just west of the courthouse. An exchange of words turned into an exchange of blows, and guns were drawn. Chiles was killed. His young son Elijah picked up his father's gun and shot Marshal Peacock. Peacock's son Charles shot and killed the Chiles boy. The whole confrontation was tragic and typical of an era when so much anger and bitterness stifled progress and healing.

In 1866, Greene County, Missouri, saw the last of the Federal troops stationed at Springfield leave for home. Almost immediately, there followed a period of increased lawlessness, as horse theft, robbery and even murder were becoming more commonplace. A group of men calling themselves the "Regulators" or the "Honest Men's League" was organized at Walnut Grove. Within a few weeks, the group shot one man, lynched three more and helped the sheriff locate and arrest seven more. The Regulators then rode on to the Springfield square and held a rally, giving speeches justifying their organization and its actions. Whatever the motives, the effect was to drive the growing criminal element out of the area for fear of the group. In county after county, returning Confederate soldiers found themselves at odds with the law. As the guerrillas and state guard were not considered legitimate combatants, they were liable for civil prosecution for crimes committed during the war. The Jayhawkers and Federal soldiers, however, were exempt from such penalties. The weight of the Radical Republican government bore down on many in Missouri and only drove a deeper wedge between communities that had supported opposing sides in the war.

Many Missourians moved south and west, hoping for more favorable conditions. Lewis Dalton and his wife, Adeline (Younger) Dalton, moved their family from Belton to Indian Territory. Belle Shirley's family left Carthage for Scyene, Texas. During the war, Martha Jane Canary's family had left Princeton, Missouri, for Montana. For those who supported the guerrillas or the South and stayed, the next several years would leave memories almost as bitter as the years of warfare. As posses and lynch mobs thinned their ranks, the ex-guerrillas turned outlaws would have little trouble finding new recruits from the impoverished and marginalized Missourians of southern background. Young men whose families had power and position prior to the war found themselves being treated as second-class citizens. Poorer families with social and economic ties to the old order were also marginalized. The old local banks were being gobbled up by institutions owned by Union supporters and by national banks, as laws were enacted to favor the latter. These banks accelerated foreclosures, in part to increase deposits to a level that would give them the favored national bank status. But this had the effect of pushing many of the old families off their land. The banks, stagecoach lines and railroads were largely owned by eastern and pro-Union businessmen.

Regardless of their true motives in robbing these businesses, the outlaws found support in many communities for doing harm to the "enemy." John Newman Edwards in the *Kansas City Times* and in dime novels would extol the virtues of the young men driven to outlawry by the evil banks and railroads and Radical Republican government. Ex-guerrillas including the James brothers were accused of robbing the Judge John McClain Banking House in Savannah, Missouri, in March 1867. That same month, a gang robbed the Hughes and Wasson Bank of Richmond; again, the James brothers and the Youngers were suspects. In March 1868, the gang was accused of robbing the Nimrod Long Banking Company of Russellville, Kentucky. In December 1869, the James brothers were identified as the robbers of the Daviess County Savings Bank in Gallatin, Missouri. As they were riding from town, Jesse was thrown from his horse and dragged with a foot caught in the stirrup. He got loose, but the horse ran off, and he had to ride double with Frank. On their way out of town, they stole a horse from Daniel Smoote at gunpoint. Smoote later successfully sued Jesse (Jesse sent a lawyer but declined to show up in court himself to reply to the suit). Smoote had corralled Jesse's ride, and after Jesse's lawyer withdrew his defense, the court awarded Smoote Jesse's horse, which was believed to be of Kentucky racing stock and worth nearly three times the value of Smoote's horse. A $3,000 reward for the capture of Frank and Jesse for the killing of cashier John Sheets was offered, but few who knew the dangerous gunmen were optimistic about living to collect or to spend it. It was believed that Jesse mistook John Sheets for Samuel Cox, who had killed Bloody Bill Anderson. Two men the brothers spoke with in nearby Kidder reported that Jesse claimed to be Anderson's brother and that he had just killed his killer.

In June 1871, four members of the gang robbed the Ocobock Brothers Bank in Corydon, Iowa. In response, the bank retained the services of the Pinkerton Detective Agency. The firm was established in 1850 by Allan Pinkerton and served as private security for President Lincoln and later as contract investigators for the U.S. Department of Justice. The agency provided spies and strikebreakers for railroads and other corporations against union organizers, as well as security guards for people and their valuables, even offering armed men as private military contractors. The James Gang was a particular thorn in Pinkerton's side, as the company had little luck in bringing the gang to justice. The Pinkerton Agency had successfully taken down the Reno Gang (the first non-wartime train robbers) by sending founding member John Reno to the Missouri State Penitentiary for the 1867 robbery of the Daviess County Courthouse and breaking up the rest of the gang the next year. In April 1872, members of the James-Younger Gang robbed the Bank of Columbia in Columbia, Kentucky. In September 1872, Jesse James and two other gang members boldly robbed the Kansas City Exposition ticket office at the fair, netting $8,000. A little girl's leg was injured either by a stray bullet or by being stepped on by one of the bandits' horses as they dashed away. In October, the *Kansas City Times* published a letter purported to be from the three robbers claiming hurt feelings at being called thieves, as that put them on a par with President Ulysses S. Grant and his party. The letter claimed that Grant and the Republicans robbed from the poor and gave to the rich, while the outlaws robbed from the rich and gave to the poor. An apology and offer to pay the medical expenses for the injured girl rounded out the letter, which was signed: Dick Turpin, Jack Shepherd and Claude Duvall (the names of three historical highwaymen).

The legend was in the public square now and quickly became a part of political discourse, a hammer for the Democrats to pound the policies of the Radical Republicans with and a means to justify defiance to Reconstruction

Right: Calamity Jane (Martha Jane Canary). *Courtesy Library of Congress: LC-USZ62-50004.*

Below: Stagecoach robbery cartoon. *Courtesy Library of Congress: LC-DIG-ppmsca-28901.*

and to change the narrative. The guerrillas-turned-outlaws were now class warriors and social reformers with guns, and seeing the practical advantage, they embraced the role. In May 1873, four members of the gang robbed the Ste. Genevieve Savings Bank in Ste. Genevieve, Missouri. In July, the gang tried their hand at train robbery. Near Adair, Iowa, they wrecked a Chicago, Rock Island and Pacific train, overturning the engine and killing the engineer in the process. In January 1874, the gang robbed a stagecoach near Hot Springs, Arkansas, taking cash and jewelry valued at $3,000. A watch of one of the passengers was among the effects found in Jesse James's possession at his death. Later that month, five to seven gang members robbed the St. Louis, Iron Mountain & Southern Railroad train at Gads Hill, Missouri. In March 1874, Pinkerton detectives were sent out to try and capture the James brothers and the Youngers. Detective Joseph Whicher set out on March 10 to take in Jesse and Frank and was found dead, shot three times, on March 11. On March 17, Pinkerton detectives Louis Lull and John Boyle and St. Clair County deputy sheriff Edwin P. Daniels got into a gun battle with Jim and John Younger. Lull, Daniels and John Younger were killed.

In April 1874, Jesse married his first cousin Zerelda Mimms, and the couple honeymooned in Galveston. That same month, a stagecoach robbery in Austin, Texas, was credited to members of the gang. In June 1874, Frank James married Ann Ralston. The gang was accused of robbing a stage in Missouri in August, a bank in Mississippi on December 7 and a train in Kansas the very next day (an unlikely feat). In January 1875, six Pinkerton agents, thinking the brothers were at the family farm, surrounded the home and tossed a smoke bomb into the house. Archie Samuel (the James brothers' nine-year-old half brother) thought the bomb was a stick that fell out of the fireplace and tossed it back in. It exploded, killing him and taking off the lower part of their mother's arm. The Pinkerton reputation with the public was badly damaged by the incident. Allan Pinkerton's son William Allan Pinkerton was working as an agent at the time, and he indicated that the agency's frustration with the case grew alongside the James family legend.

Jesse Edwards James (Jesse James's son) was born in August 1875. In September, the gang was accused of robbing the Huntington Bank in Huntington, West Virginia. In July 1876, the gang robbed a Missouri-Pacific train at Rockey Cut, Missouri. In September, the gang was nearly destroyed in the botched attempt to rob the First National Bank of Northfield, Minnesota. It was as if the gang forgot all they had learned about the business. They came into town dressed conspicuously in long overcoats riding expensive

Pat Connell
Special Agent
Southern Express Co.

William A. Pinkerton

Sam Finley
Asst. Special Agent
Southern Express Co.

William A. Pinkerton (*center*) and railroad agents. *Courtesy Library of Congress: LC- DIG-ppmsca-10781.*

Allan Pinkerton, founder of Pinkerton Detective Agency. *Courtesy Library of Congress C-USZ62-117576.*

saddle horses. One member fired his pistol before everyone was in place. In addition, the gang had chosen a target far from their base of operations and supportive friends and neighbors. The list of mistakes goes on and on. The bank cashier refused to open the safe and ended up shot. The town erupted, killing gang members Clell Miller and Bill Chadwell and wounding Jim, Bob and Cole Younger. The Youngers and Charlie Pitts escaped, but Pitts was killed and the Youngers were further shot up when a posse caught up with them later. Jesse and Frank escaped unharmed and managed to elude thousands of reward seekers, lawmen and posses and return to Missouri. Again, the legend grew.

In the next three years, Frank's son Robert Franklin James and Jesse's daughter Mary Susan James were born. It wasn't until October 1879 that the gang would try another big score, hitting the Chicago, Alton & St. Louis train at Glendale, Missouri, and netting $40,000. In September 1880, the gang robbed a stagecoach in Mammoth Springs, Kentucky. In March 1881, the gang robbed a paymaster leaving a bank in Muscle Shoals, Alabama. In July, they hit the Chicago, Rock Island & Pacific train at Winston, Missouri. In September, the gang made its last big score, robbing the Chicago & Alton train at Blue Cut near Glendale.

Most of the old guerrillas by that time were dead, in jail or had found a way back into society. Jesse kept moving, living across the alley from the father of the Jackson County sheriff for a while. With his hair dyed and his beard grown out, and dressing the part of a much older man, Jesse would chat with the posses gathered there about their plans to ride out to look for him and his gang. He moved to St. Joseph, Missouri, in November, renting a house under the last name Howard. While living there, he moved about freely, even cutting into a parade with Jesse Jr. sitting on the saddle in front of him. Bob Ford had been a hanger-on with the gang and had been friends with Dick Liddel. When Liddel and Jesse James's cousin Wood Hite got into an argument-turned-shootout, Ford took Liddel's side and killed Hite. Ford was arrested. Facing death from the hangman or from Jesse if he found out

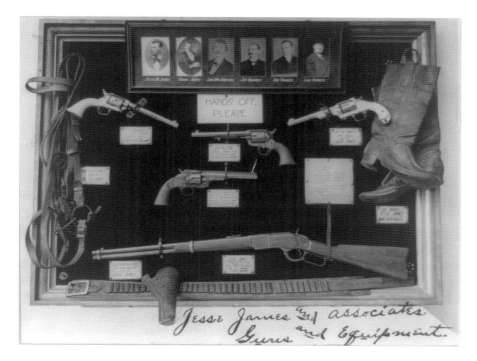

James Gang guns. *Courtesy Library of Congress: LC-USZ62-7777.*

he'd killed his cousin, Ford offered the authorities Jesse James. Governor of Missouri Thomas Crittenden offered Ford a pardon for murdering Hite and a promise of a pardon and a $10,000 reward for killing Jesse James. On April 3, 1882, Bob and Charlie Ford came to Jesse's home and discussed the possibility of robbing the Platte City, Missouri bank. Neither had a great deal of experience, but the gang was so depleted that Jesse was willing to take a chance with them. Jesse turned his back to the Fords for a moment to adjust a framed needlepoint picture on the wall. Bob Ford drew his gun and shot and killed him. Jesse James was only thirty-eight.

Frank James turned his gun over to Governor Crittenden on October 5, 1882. He would face a number of trials and accusations but was never convicted of any of the gang's crimes. Crittenden was roundly criticized for his part in using public funds to pay for the assassination of a private citizen who had not been convicted of any capital offense. Bob and Charlie Ford were arrested and convicted and pardoned, though it appears they received little of the reward money promised for killing James. Charlie committed suicide after a couple of years looking over his shoulder expecting to see

Home in St. Joseph where Jesse James was assassinated. *Courtesy Library of Congress.*

Frank James. Bob ended up in Creede, Colorado, a failure at acting and the saloon business. He was killed by a shotgun blast from Edward O'Kelley. The motive was unknown, but since O'Kelley had lived in Missouri and was married to a relative of the Youngers, many have assumed it may have had something to do with Ford killing James. Governor Crittenden was vilified by many, and former Confederate colonel John S. Marmaduke was elected the forty-fifth governor of the state. Marmaduke was the nephew of Claiborne Jackson and a native Missourian who in 1863 had killed his commanding officer (Brigadier General Lucius M. Walker) in a duel and had commanded a brigade in Price's invasion of Missouri. He was the perfect Missouri replacement for former Union general Crittenden.

The James Gang had many imitators; doubtless some of the crimes attributed to them were committed by others. In the 1880s, the Durbin Gang in Lafayette County, Missouri, robbed several trains by buying tickets, sneaking back to the freight cars, breaking in and pushing freight off to gang members waiting in the woods alongside the tracks. The train riders would close up the freight cars, re-take their seats and get off at the next town. The railroad would have no idea that the robbery took place until the cars were opened in St. Louis or Chicago. I found out that my wife is related to

John S. Marmaduke, ex-Confederate and postwar governor of Missouri. *Courtesy Library of Congress: LC-DIG-cwpb-06001.*

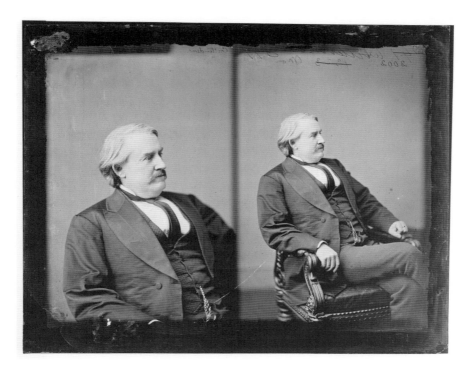

Governor T.T. Crittenden. *Courtesy Library of Congress: LC-DIG-cwpbh-04801.*

some of the members of this gang. It took the railroad detectives quite some time to catch them. The combination of boldness and careful planning, along with local support, made Missouri outlaws a major headache for the railroads and banks.

Most supporters of the Confederacy in Missouri were not guerrillas and did not join outlaw gangs after the war. A fairly large number left the state, and more than one thousand left the United States entirely—for a while. Some surrendered, some wouldn't. Joseph Orville Shelby was born in 1830 into a wealthy family. Raised in Kentucky; he attended Transylvania University and then became a rope manufacturer until 1852. He moved to Waverly, Missouri, and engaged in the steamboat business, raised hemp and owned a sawmill and a rope works. During the Border War, he led a group of Ruffians, and after the Camp Jackson Affair, he formed the Lafayette County Mounted Rifles to serve in the Missouri State Guard. He was elected captain and led the group at Carthage, Wilson's Creek and Pea Ridge. In 1862, he was promoted to colonel and slipped into Missouri to recruit a cavalry regiment, which he did and brought them through Union lines to Arkansas. He was given a brigade of newly recruited regiments. In the fall of 1863, Shelby led them on a 1,500-mile raid through Missouri, causing one thousand Union casualties and carrying off or destroying more than $2 million in federal supplies or property. On his return, he was promoted to brigadier general. In Arkansas, he helped thwart Union general Frederick Steele's Camden expedition by harassing and attacking his supply lines, which forced Steele to retreat to Little Rock. Shelby commanded a brigade in Sterling Price's ill-fated raid of 1864, distinguishing himself at the battles of Little Blue River and Westport and repeatedly putting himself and his men between Price's pursuers and the retreating force as they skulked back to Arkansas. After Lee's surrender, he went to Mexico with one thousand men rather than surrender. Shelby returned to Missouri in 1867 and resumed farming. In 1893, he was actually appointed U.S. marshal for the Western District of Missouri. He held court in Kansas City, with many old Rebels and former Union adversaries who had grown to respect the man coming by to visit. During the 1894 Pullman Strike, he helped to preserve order while presiding over a large contingent of deputy marshals. After the Civil War, Shelby and many of his troops simply avoided and outlasted the Federals, never formally surrendering yet managing to return to successful civilian lives.

My wife and I used to take my mother-in-law on drives into eastern Jackson County when she was in her eighties. She had grown up in the little town of Buckner and enjoyed showing us her old haunts. Each time we turned off the highway toward downtown, she would point out a stone home and say "That's Sam Chiles's house." A few years after she passed away, I was doing research for *Lockdown: Outlaws, Lawmen and Frontier Justice in Jackson County, Missouri* and came across that name I'd heard so many times before. Sam Chiles was another member of the Jackson County, Missouri clan that had supported the Confederacy during the Civil War. He had followed Shelby through the war years and down to Mexico. He returned sometime after the war and, like Shelby, avoided trouble and avoided surrender. In 1898, Sam Chiles, the unrepentant Rebel, was elected marshal of Jackson County and then was re-elected two years later. One of his deputies was a local tough who had worked as a bouncer in his older brother Jim's bar. Tom Pendergast would learn the law-and-order game from Missouri rebel Sam Chiles and would succeed him in office as the Jackson County marshal in 1902. The man who would come to be known as "Boss Tom" and would run Kansas City and to some degree Missouri politics got his start working for "undefeated" Sam Chiles. Chiles retired to his fine home in Buckner, where he was an officer in the savings and loan. A pillar of the little community my mother-in-law grew up in (her father was the town barber), Chiles lived to the ripe old age of eighty-four. His funeral was attended by a huge crowd, including, no doubt, the barber and his daughter.

SQUIRREL CAGES AND OTHER INGENIOUS INNOVATIONS

New challenges led to changes in how law enforcement was organized and how prisoners were dealt with. In larger communities, large courthouses were being built, city police forces were established and city and county jails were being utilized more. Communities like St. Joseph and Hannibal combined the courthouse and jail in one building. Steel cells and doors were being mass produced, as were entire facilities. In Gallatin, a rotating jail, dubbed a "squirrel cage," was installed in 1889. The entire cell block is made up of eight pie-shaped cells that sit on a single axis that could be turned using a crank. With only one cell door facing the entrance door and the rest facing solid walls, only the prisoners in one cell could enter or leave at a time. There was also a grub hole to pass food through, so even the one cell facing the entrance didn't have to be opened. Each section has steel bunk beds and a bathroom at the narrow end of the cell. Just eighteen rotating jails were built, and only three remain. The rotary jail and marshal's home in Gallatin, Missouri, are listed in the National Register of Historic Places. The building was used to house prisoners from 1889 until 1975 and is now a museum open to the public (by appointment only). The Daviess County Squirrel Cage Jail has a Facebook page offering additional information and tour schedules.

The Pauly Jail Building Company of St. Louis, Missouri, built prefabricated jail cells that could be transported by wagon starting in 1856. An industry leader for five generations, the manufacturer continues to make innovations in cell doors, windows and plumbing. A convenient solution, the steel cages could be moved around, set in the center of a room and were ready-made without a lot of expensive stonework. In historic Blackwater, Missouri, a mock-up of the old city jail includes a nineteenth-century prefabricated, freestanding cell. In the late nineteenth and early twentieth centuries, many jails, especially in southern or Border States, added cells to accommodate the

Steel cell, Historic Blackwater, Missouri Jail. *Author's collection.*

Squirrel Cage Jail and Marshal's Home Museum, Gallatin, Missouri. *The original uploader was Americasroof at English Wikipedia (Transferred from en.wikipedia.com to Wikipedia Commons.) [CC BY-SA 3.0 (http://creativecommons.org/licenses/by-sa/3.0)], via Wikimedia Commons.*

Cooper County Hanging Barn. *Author's collection.*

growing prison population of African Americans as the use of prison labor in the form of chain gangs became more common. The Jackson County Marshal's Home and Jail added a block of steel cells after the turn of the century but scrapped them in the Depression era. The county didn't need the cells anymore, as it had also scrapped the chain gangs that they were built to accommodate.

In Boonville, the Cooper County sheriff wanted a barn to house his wagon and horses (deputies and posse members could also keep horses there). In the nineteenth century, county sheriffs were responsible for executions of prisoners convicted in their jurisdiction, but public executions had gone out of vogue in many communities. When the barn was built, a gallows was installed inside (out of sight), with thirteen steps up to the platform and noose. The hanging barn was used well into the twentieth century, with the last prisoner climbing those stairs in the 1930s.

6

BEYOND THE BORDER

Missouri was known as the "Outlaw State," but it was more than that, supplying ready-made trouble for other states as well. A number of western outlaws and lawmen got their start in old Missouri but peaked or matured in states or territories far from home. Many Missourians had fled the state during the war and found devastation in their former home when they returned. Men who had supported the Confederacy, even if they had not taken up arms, often faced discrimination by the new order. Where opportunities for former Confederates were limited, they opened up to men from pro-Union states. Among the offerings were jobs policing the area. With the end of the war, the business of expansion, settlement and trade in the West could resume. Missouri would rise from the ashes, but many of its sons and daughters would be marked by the years of conflict. Families like the Daltons and Canarys moved west, looking for new opportunity and a new start. Union army officers who sought advancement or merely continued employment vied for positions in the West. Last but not least, young men from Missouri sought adventure and fortune on the many paths west and turned up on ranches, in mining towns and all along the trails as guides and scouts to the waves of immigrants that came after the war.

In *Dynasty of Western Outlaws*, Paul I. Wellman goes a step further than many historians in crediting Missouri as a training ground for criminals. Starting with Quantrill's core group, Wellman traces two lines of criminal gangs through the nineteenth and into the twentieth century, with at least one surviving member of each gang providing a seed for the next. Out of Quantrill's guerrillas came the James and Younger brothers, and the Daltons (cousins of the Youngers) started another gang. After the Dalton gang was decimated at Coffeeville, member Bill Doolin started a gang with Bill Dalton. The Doolin-Dalton Gang was dismantled in a huge shootout at Ingalls, Oklahoma, in 1893. However, former member of the gang Little Dick West soon joined a gang led by Al Jennings, and another gang member (Dick Howell) joined with Bill Cook in the Cook Gang. The Jennings Gang was broken up in 1898. Coming down another line, Belle Starr knew the Youngers and many of the ex-guerrillas. Her brother and first husband had fought as guerrillas. Her second husband was Sam Starr; his nephew was Henry Starr, who grew up with an uncle and aunt who were notorious bandits. Henry joined the Cook Gang and ended up in prison for a while. When he got out and got back in the business, one of his new gang members was Al Spencer. Spencer was eventually caught and jailed for stealing horses. While in jail in Oklahoma, he joined forces with Frank Nash, and the two escaped the state prison and went on a bank robbing spree. They were tied to the robberies of between twenty and forty banks. In 1933, Frank Nash was captured. On his way to trial, he was escorted by FBI agents and met by Kansas City policemen at Union Station. He was taken to a waiting car, only to be riddled with bullets by machine gun–toting criminals, including Charles Arthur "Pretty Boy" Floyd, whom Wellman also connected to the old Missouri gangs. Whether one thinks that Wellman's thesis is sound, or that the influence of Quantrill was stretched too thin by the twentieth century, a number of Missouri-born rowdies found their way into the outlaw profession all over the West for decades after Quantrill's death.

Tom Horn was born on a farm in Scotland County, Missouri, in 1860. He headed west as a teenager and worked as a civilian scout and translator for the army. He took part in the Apache Wars and the capture of Geronimo and went on to work as a range detective for the Pinkerton Agency. He served in the Spanish-American War as chief packer of the Fifth Corps. While serving in that capacity, he saw the assault on San Juan Hill by the Rough Riders and came under fire, as well as catching yellow fever. Horn ended up working as a hired gun for the Wyoming Stock Men's Association and was hanged for allegedly killing a fourteen-year-old boy from a family of sheep farmers. The case had a lot of holes in it, but by the time it came to trial, the cattlemen apparently found him expendable and put little effort into his defense. He was convicted and hanged in 1903.

Myra Mae Belle Shirley was born and raised in Carthage, Missouri. Her father's business holdings covered most of a city block downtown. She graduated from the Carthage Female Academy, where she had received a classical education and learned to play piano. Unfortunately for Belle, her family was on the wrong side of history. Her brother became a bushwhacker and was killed; her first husband, Jim Reed, had been a Confederate guerrilla. After the war, Belle's family moved to Scyene, Texas, where she and Jim Reed were married. They had two children (Pearl and Ed), but Jim had run afoul of the law and was killed in a shootout. Eventually, Belle got together with Cherokee outlaw Sam Starr. She lived in Indian Territory in what is now Oklahoma and made an income from selling stolen horses (often stolen by ex-guerrillas). In 1883, she was arrested and convicted of horse theft and was sentenced to nine months in prison by Judge Isaac Parker. Sam Starr died in a shootout with his lawman/cousin Frank West in 1886, leaving Belle and her children in a quandary. Since Belle was no longer married to a member of the tribe, she had no claim to the land and home she was living in. She soon remedied the problem by marrying a much younger member of the Creek tribe named Jim July. Belle associated with dozens of criminals and ex-guerrillas and had a number of enemies. She was murdered in 1889, bushwhacked, then executed. The case is still considered unsolved. The same year she was killed, dime novelist Richard K. Fox published *Belle Starr, the Bandit Queen, or The Female Jesse James*.

Belle Starr (with Blue Duck). *Courtesy Wikimedia Commons.*

John Harris Behan was born in Westport, Missouri, in 1845. As a young man, he moved to California and during the Civil War worked as a civilian employee of Carleton's Column of Union Volunteers, taking part in the Battle of Apache Pass in 1862. After the war, he moved to Arizona Territory and served in various government positions while trying his hand at mining and other speculative ventures. He was appointed sheriff of Cochise County when Wyatt Earp stepped down from the position, and Tombstone was in his jurisdiction when the "Gunfight at the OK Corral" took place. He has been portrayed as a foil to Wyatt Earp or a tool of the cowboys, but he was, like many of Missouri's exports, not all bad all the time. He worked in various public positions, performing effectively in some and being accused of corruption in others. He served his country in the Spanish-American War and the Boxer Rebellion but died of complications from syphilis at age sixty-nine.

Newman Clanton (patriarch of the gang known as the "Cowboys") moved to Callaway County, Missouri, and was married there in 1841. Three of the couple's older boys—Tom, Phin and Ike Clanton—were born in Callaway County and spent their early childhoods there. Newman moved the family to Illinois in late 1851, and eventually—by way of Texas and California—they ended up in Arizona Territory. There, the family business included rustling cattle, robbing stagecoaches and teamsters and engaging in violent activities.

Harvey Logan (a.k.a. "Kid Curry") was orphaned at age nine. He and his three brothers then moved in with an aunt in Dodson, Missouri. He stayed with the aunt into his teen years then got work as a ranch hand. He worked with a man called "Flat Nose" George Curry. Logan at some point started using the name Curry, and it stuck. Kid Curry left ranch life to become an outlaw, joining the Black Jack Ketchum Gang, and he later became a member of Butch Cassidy and the Sundance Kid's Wild Bunch.

Johnny Ringo grew up near Gallatin, Missouri, worked his way west and ended up as a member of the Cowboys outside of Tombstone. He has been portrayed as a gunfighter and foil to Wyatt Earp and Doc Holliday in several movies, including *Tombstone* (1993).

Henry Newton Brown was raised near Rolla, Missouri, by his aunt and uncle. Born in 1857, he grew up in a state torn apart by war and financially depressed in the aftermath. At age seventeen, he headed west, working as a cowboy in Colorado and Texas and finally ending up in Lincoln County, New Mexico Territory. He became a member of a group of young gunmen known as the "Regulators" who worked for rancher John Tunstall. After Tunstall was killed, Brown, William Henry McCarty (a.k.a. "Billy the

Five members of the Wild Bunch. *Courtesy Wikimedia Commons.*

Pinkerton identifier card on train robber Will Roberts, member of the Wild Bunch. *Courtesy Library of Congress: LC-DIG-ppmsca-10791.*

Kid") and other members of the group took revenge by killing Lincoln County sheriff William Brady. They were involved in a number of deadly shootouts, including the siege at the home of Tunstall's partner, Alexander McSween. Brown and several members of the group, including Billy the Kid, managed to fight their way out despite being greatly outnumbered and the house they were in set on fire. Brown and the other Regulators stole some cattle and took them to Texas, where he stayed, working as a lawman for a while in Oldham County. However, he was dismissed for his hot temper. He worked various cowboy jobs in Oklahoma Territory then ended up back in law enforcement as assistant marshal of Caldwell, Kansas, in 1882. Later elected and then re-elected marshal, Brown and his deputy, Texas outlaw Ben Wheeler, cleaned up the wild cattle town. Taking part in a number of shootouts, Brown's defeat of two gunmen at once earned him praise in the *Caldwell Post* as "one of the quickest men on the trigger in the Southwest." Seemingly established, Brown bought a house in town, got married and settled into his position as marshal. But he and Wheeler weren't ready to give up the outlaw life entirely. In 1884, Brown, Wheeler and two other men were caught by a posse after trying to rob the Medicine Valley Bank in Medicine Lodge, Kansas. The bank president and a cashier had been shot, and the safe was closed before the robbers could get any money. Brown and his gang were arrested and placed in jail. A lynch mob formed, and Brown ran past them as his cell was opened. He was cut in half with a blast from a shotgun. The other three prisoners, including a wounded member of the gang, were hanged by the mob.

Lewis Dalton and his wife, Adeline Younger Dalton (aunt to the Younger brothers of the James-Younger Gang), left Jackson County for Indian Territory in 1882. The couple had twelve sons and three daughters. Most of the children were born in Missouri. Older brother Frank became a deputy U.S. marshal but was killed in the line of duty in 1887. Lewis Dalton passed away in 1889, leaving Adeline to raise the remaining children of their fifteen-member clan. Brothers Bob, Grat and Emmett all worked in law enforcement at some level early on, but Emmett worked mostly as a cowboy. The Missouri and Kansas cowboys he worked with would form a pool of recruits for the gang the young men later formed. After a dispute with a federal marshal over not being paid the little salary they were owed, the Daltons tried to make money illegally by selling liquor in the Osage Nation in 1890. With warrants out for their arrest, the brothers, along with a few of the cowboys with whom Emmett had worked, started a criminal gang that successfully robbed trains over the next two years They failed, however, in their first attempt in California. Bill and Grat were arrested; Grat got life in prison but later escaped while being transported by stealing a handcuff key and jumping out the window of a moving train. The core of the gang got the hang of robbing trains and made off with more than $20,000 in their next four train robberies. Finally, with gang members Bill Powers and Dick Broadwell, the Daltons made the brazen but foolhardy move of trying to rob both the Condon and First National Banks in Coffeeville, Kansas. The fiasco that followed left the marshal, three townsmen and four gang members dead and two citizens and one gang member wounded.

Hyman G. Neill (a.k.a. "Hoodoo Brown") was from Lexington, Missouri. His family moved to Warrensburg, Missouri, after the Civil War. He was working for a printer but apparently wasn't enjoying the job. One day, after being told to get some rags to clean with, he walked out and jumped a train that passed by the office's back door and shouted that he was going to get "your durn rags" as the train hauled him away. Hoodoo drifted west, ending up in Las Vegas, New Mexico Territory, as justice of the peace and leading a group called the Dodge City Gang. Robbing stagecoaches and trains, committing murders and thefts and using bribes and intimidation, they gained control over municipal affairs. Hoodoo had secured the positions of justice of the peace and coroner and installed members of the gang on the coroner's jury. The stacked jury ruled that the cause of death of the gang's victims was not homicide, and the defendants thus could avert prosecution. Members of the notorious group included deputy U.S. marshals, the city marshal and various hard cases like David Rutabaugh (a.k.a. "Dirty Dave Rudabaugh") and David Mather (a.k.a. "Mysterious Dave Mather"). After two years of running the town, a vigilante group challenged their dominance, threatening the group with death if they didn't leave town. Brown moved on

Dalton Gang members (photo taken after botched Coffeeville robbery). *Courtesy Wikimedia Commons.*

to Texas, then Mexico. At some point after his death, his body was returned to Missouri and buried in Lexington.

As the Democratic Party began to regain some of its power in Missouri, former Rebels found it easier to re-enter society. Old animosities died slowly, but the country was back on the move. Railroads were spreading across the country, connecting markets and produce. Though some ex-Rebels, like the James Gang, had managed to gain some sympathy in the press, the general public and the business community were ready to move forward. Attacking banks and railroads didn't help merchants who kept their money in the bank or farmers who shipped their goods by rail. Riding in and shooting up a town, maybe killing an innocent bystander with a stray bullet wasn't part of a noble cause to the average citizen. Not every group of outlaws had a code or made distinctions as to who they would or wouldn't rob. Towns began hiring sheriffs and deputies with military experience, men who wouldn't back down and were a better match for the gangs.

James Butler Hickok came to the Missouri-Kansas border area around 1856. At various times, he worked and lived on both sides of the border.

He ended up joining Senator James Lane's "army" of Free Staters and eventually became Lane's personal bodyguard. In 1858, he was elected constable of Monticello, Kansas (a tiny trail town just west of Kansas City). By 1860, he was working out of Independence, Missouri, driving freight wagons on the Santa Fe Trail. While working in that capacity, he was badly mauled by a bear and ended up being put on light duty by the freight company in a station in Nebraska Territory. A confrontation at that post led to a shootout between Hickok and three other men. Hickok won, killing all three. Somewhere around that time, he started going by William Hickok (his father's name).

Wild Bill Hickok. *Courtesy Wikimedia Commons.*

When the Civil War began, Hickok joined the Union army and served as a soldier, spy, wagon driver, deputy to the Springfield provost marshal and scout. Hickok was already building a larger-than-life reputation during this period. In Independence, a bartender had won a fair fight with a local man, but the man's family and friends gathered to exact retribution. Hickok stepped between the man and the crowd and said that he would kill anyone who touched the bartender. No one in the crowd had the nerve to test him. As the crowd dispersed, a woman shouted, "Good for you, Wild Bill!"

After the war, Hickok, who had worked as a police detective for the provost marshal there, returned to Springfield and was making a living as a professional gambler. In a card game with fellow gambler and ex-Confederate Davis Tutt, he had bet and lost more than he had. Tutt grabbed Hickok's watch as collateral for the remainder of the debt. Hickok warned him not to wear it in public. Tutt kept the watch, and he and his friends goaded Hickok about the debt. Finally, Tutt bragged that he would wear the watch in the public square. Hickok warned him not to do it or face the consequences. Tutt and Wild Bill faced off in the public square on July 21, 1865. Both men drew their guns. Tutt missed; Hickok didn't. The story, along with several others about Wild Bill, made it into the eastern papers. A writer for *Harper's New Monthly Magazine* interviewed Hickok several times and wrote an article that appeared in the February 1867 issue. A star was born. Leaving Springfield for Kansas City, Hickok worked off and on as a civilian scout for the army (including for George Armstrong Custer) and as a deputy U.S. marshal.

In 1866, Hickok demonstrated his ability to bring peace to fractious situations. Kansas City, Missouri, had a baseball team called the Antelopes. They were intense rivals with the team from Atchison. The umpires at the two previous games had been pelted with dirt clods and potatoes, and one literally had to run for his life. Someone had to be found to umpire the next game. On August 12, 1866, James Butler Hickok stepped onto the field. One of the politest, least contested games in history was played. Hickok wore his set of Colt revolvers on his hips throughout the contest, which the Antelopes won, 48–38. It was reported that the crowd was as quiet as if they were at a prayer meeting. Though Hickok wasn't born in Missouri and was an enemy combatant to some in the state, he spent several formative years in Missouri or just across the border in Kansas and learned how to handle Missouri's rough crowds. He would go on to work in law enforcement in the

Calamity Jane at Wild Bill's grave. *Courtesy Library of Congress: LC-DIG-ds-05300.*

Wyatt Earp. *Courtesy Wikimedia Commons.*

booming Kansas cow towns and even did a stint trying to act with Bill Cody. But Hickok was more comfortable out west. He was gambling and gold prospecting in Deadwood, South Dakota, when he was murdered by Jack McCall. He was buried there, and years later, Martha Jane Canary (a.k.a. "Calamity Jane"), who always claimed to have had a close relationship with Hickok, was buried next to him.

Virgil Earp served three years in the Union army. His brother Wyatt was too young and stayed home to hunt game and help provide for the family. The Earps moved to Lamar, Missouri, in 1870, where Virgil married Rosetta Dragoo and Wyatt married Urilla Sutherland. Wyatt began his law enforcement career as constable of the little town. Like Hickok, these young men had come west to seek their fortune and found work policing the border towns that were trying to rebuild in the aftermath of war. Wyatt's wife died of typhoid the first year of their marriage, and he had a down period where he had multiple run-ins with the law. He moved on to work policing Kansas cow towns and became famous for his feud with the Cowboys (a group of outlaws whose leaders came from Missouri) in Tombstone, Arizona.

This short list is not meant to imply that all of the bad guys in the Old West came from Missouri. Rather, a fair share of Missouri-born or Missouri-"educated" outlaws and lawmen ended up making their mark out west.

WALLS THAT TALK

In 1838, Missouri built its own penitentiary, opening its doors to fifteen prisoners. During the nineteenth century, the prison expanded to accommodate a couple of thousand residents. The addition, known as A-hall, was built in 1868 and housed inmates until the day the prison closed in 2004. Referred to by prisoners as "The Walls" because of the massive stone blocks that surround the prison, the Missouri State Penitentiary (MSP) in Jefferson City, Missouri, earned a reputation as the bloodiest forty-seven acres in America, as executions, riots and killings took place within the facility over the course of its 160-plus-year run of service. With imposing stone buildings that housed some of Missouri's most notorious criminals, the penitentiary looks like a fortress. MSP closed its doors in 2004, only to re-open as a popular tourist destination. The MSP museum is located at the Colonel Darwin W. Marmaduke House (the former warden's home), a fine two-story brick home that houses displays providing information on several aspects of prison life, including a replica cell. Tours can be arranged by contacting www.MissouriPenTours.com or calling toll-free (866) 998-6998. The season runs from March to November.

One of the earliest denizens of the prison was John Reno, one of the founding members of the Reno Gang. Bill Ryan of the James-Younger Gang spent time as a guest there. Infamous inmates of the twentieth century included criminals from Pretty Boy Floyd to James Earl Ray, who escaped by hiding in a truck transporting bread from the prison bakery. Ray went on to assassinate Martin Luther King the next year. Heavyweight champion boxer Sonny Liston learned his trade while serving time at the penitentiary. The prisoners manufactured shoes and built homes in the nineteenth century, and the largest saddletree factory in the world was based there.

Now the doors to "The Walls" are open to the public. Guided history tours of various lengths are available by appointment. One can learn about the facility in detail and take photographs of the many sights there. Student tours include history tours, photography tours and ghost tours.

Missouri State Penitentiary. *By CosmiCataclysm (Own work) [CC BY-SA 3.0 (http://creativecommons.org/licenses/by-sa/3.0)], via Wikimedia Commons.*

Ghost tours, ghost hunts and a ghost hunting class are available, as are overnight paranormal investigations for individuals and for paranormal groups. A facility like this that is still standing and available for public viewing is a rare commodity, and the state is fortunate and wise to make such good use of it.

7

ORNERY OZARKS

Before the Civil War, southwest Missouri was unsettled. After the war, the region continued to be unsettled. Mining towns and frontier communities tucked away in the hills were generally small and sporadically dangerous. In Taney County, there were forty murders between 1865 and 1885, with no convictions. In 1885, a group of citizens met at Snapp's Balds, a treeless hilltop near Kirbyville, Missouri, where they discussed how to bring law and order back to Taney County. From that meeting the fearsome group got its name: the Bald Knobbers. The group's leader, Nathaniel Kinney, was a Springfield, Missouri saloon owner and preacher. The group's members had mostly supported the Union during the war. They lashed "sinners" for engaging in arson, stealing hogs and, especially, committing adultery. The group lynched Frank and Tubal Taylor for wounding one of their members. The vigilantes would toss bundles of switches on porches as a warning that the home's residents might face a "slicking" if they didn't move out. An anti-vigilante group whose members were mostly Democrats and had favored the South in the war formed to counter the Bald Knobbers. Knowing they would have to kill Kinney to break the vigilantes, five men sat down to a game of poker. The loser would have to turn assassin. Billy Miles lost the game. Nate Kinney was conducting inventory at a store for the court when Miles walked in and shot him. Miles dropped his gun, stepped outside and claimed self-defense. The story gained national attention, and Miles was exonerated.

"Justice Asleep," anti-vigilante cartoon in *Puck. Courtesy Library of Congress: LC-DIG-ppmsca-28402.*

The sparsely populated counties in southern Missouri all had a similar problem after the war. Keeping order was difficult, as local governments could be just as corrupt and often less effective than the vigilante groups. The Bald Knobbers of Taney County were soon eclipsed by the Bald Knobbers of Christian County, which became so strong that local law enforcement could not control them. A militia was called, and eighty members of the Christian County chapter were arrested. Ultimately, four members were sentenced to be hanged in May 1889: Dave Walker, Billy Walker, Deacon John Mathews and Wiley Mathews. Wiley managed to escape from jail, but the other three were subjected to a botched hanging, in which the ropes were too long and the men's feet touched ground. At one point, one of the ropes broke while a prisoner was still alive, and he had to be re-hanged. The county officials were roundly criticized for the poorly executed execution, and the bitterness between the vigilantes and anti-vigilantes hung around long after the hanging.

Back in Taney County, Sheriff G.E. Branson had hired bounty hunter Ed Funk to track down Billy Miles, who, though he'd avoided conviction, was still seen as an enemy to the Bald Knobbers' supporters. When the sheriff and bounty hunter found Miles at an Independence Day picnic near Kirbyville, a melee broke out, as Bald Knobbers and anti–Bald Knobbers joined in. Branson and Funk were killed. Miles and his brothers fled the area entirely. The opposing sides feuded off and on for years, and masked groups enforcing morals were reported well into the next century.

In 1907, religious author Harold Bell Wright wrote a fictional story about life in the hill country of southern Missouri. In it, he portrayed the leader of the vigilantes (Wash Gibbs) as an animalistic and violent man opposed by the peaceful protagonist (Minister Daniel Howitt). The story was ultimately published in several languages and was adapted to film four times, including a 1941 version with John Wayne. Near Branson, Missouri, the outdoor drama was presented every season beginning in 1960. *The Shepherd of the Hills* portrays the Bald Knobbers as a fearsome group of men on horseback using torches to set fire to a log cabin, which they did at every performance. The play ran from 1960 to 2017.

Joel Pinkney Fagg, known as "Pink Fagg," went to the Missouri penitentiary in 1876 for attempting to rob a shop in Springfield by throwing a container of chloroform into the attached room where the shop owner was sleeping, hoping it would keep him from waking and hearing Fagg in the store. The plan was a failure, and Pink was caught. After serving a year and a half in the penitentiary, Pink moved to Joplin and, with his brother Bud, was

Above: Execution of Carrol Rice, 1899. Hanging by county sheriff. By Lewis A. Simpson. P0771, 023083-2. *Courtesy The State Historical Society of Missouri Photograph Collection.*

Right: *The Shepherd of the Hills*, published by the Book Supply Company, Chicago, 1907. *(http://archive.org/details/ shepherdofhills1wrig). Public domain, via Wikimedia Commons.*

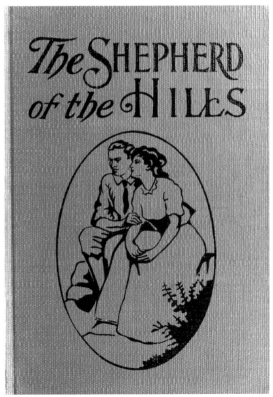

involved in gambling and illegal liquor sales. He was accused of shooting his ex-wife in 1881, but no one showed up to testify against him. In 1885, Pink shot a bartender and ended up back in the state pen. Out again, Pink shot former Confederate Major Alexander Doran in Fort Smith, Arkansas, and went to prison in Little Rock, serving just four years. After that, his trail through the newspapers and prison system seems to have gone cold. Southwest Missouri seemed like a particularly good area to disappear into. More than one criminal disappeared into those woods, whether on purpose or with masked riders dragging them there.

Outlaws in southwest Missouri knew they could end up on the wrong end of a rope or "lost" in the woods. It took strong-willed leaders to hold gangs together. In the same way that Nate Kinney inspired the fear and loyalty of the Bald Knobbers, Bud Blount led his own criminal gang, ready to take on all comers. When a member of Blount's gang was jailed for being drunk and disorderly in Webb City, the gang tried to intimidate the jailor into letting him out by shooting up the jail. The jailor didn't budge. The gang member was kept overnight, and he paid his fine and was released the next day. The group reunited in Carterville, got drunk and went back to Webb City, but they were turned back by a posse. Blount caught some buckshot during the brief shoot-out before they fled. Instead of calling it quits, the gang acquired Spencer rifles and carbines and rode back into town. They began shooting out windows and killing livestock. Firing an estimated two hundred rounds, the men wounded five people then rode out of town uninjured. Blount would be in and out of jail for manslaughter and miscellaneous other charges for years. The bad man and his followers would intimidate and prey on ordinary citizens and be a headache for law enforcement for years.

The line between lawman and criminal was sometimes blurred in communities where the sheriff had to deal with extended clans and lifelong associations between members of criminal gangs. To be a small-town or county sheriff was to walk a fine line. If you were law-and-order tough, you created enemies who might vote you out of a job. If you turned a blind eye, the good citizens would also be after you. Tough criminals called for tough men, and not all tough men were morally upright. George Hudson's father was the marshal in Granby, Missouri, and his brothers served as deputies. George had killed five men in four separate incidents. He was acquitted or simply not indicted for several crimes because witnesses ended up injured or intimidated out of testifying. It seemed to be common knowledge that he was a dangerous criminal, but with the law seeming to cover for him, nothing could be done. Hudson's mistake was getting in trouble away from home. In August 1892, lawman William Rabedew was sent to take George Hudson in on warrants from Colorado. Hudson was in a saloon, and when a Joplin policeman who was with Rabedew told Hudson he was under arrest, Hudson said, "not by a damn sight" and swung a beer bottle at the officer and reached for his gun. Rabedew drew his own gun and shot Hudson once in the head. The Joplin paper announced, "The Killer, Killed."

Southwest Missouri, the Ozark Mountains in Arkansas and southern Missouri and the Cookson Hills in Oklahoma all provided shelter for criminal gangs well into the twentieth century. Joplin was known as a "cooling off" town where criminals could lie low while the law was looking for them. Joplin was located close to the Kansas and the Oklahoma borders, and it was easy to jump out of one jurisdiction into another if law enforcement was getting too close. With lots of little towns and poor people to befriend, a somewhat smart criminal could flash money that would get him nowhere in the cities and be well fed and well hidden for weeks out in the country. The tactics of scouting a target, using surprise attacks, planning routes of escape, using superior firepower and mobility, bribing local officials or citizens and hiding among them were used by Missouri outlaws well beyond the days of Quantrill, because they worked more often than not.

Every county history in Missouri has a tale or two that adds to the picture of who its people were and are. A story from northeast Missouri, though tragic, tends to bring wry smiles and knowing nods from people all over the state. Ken McElroy was the town bully in tiny Skidmore, Missouri. He was an eighth-grade dropout who had been accused of rustling cattle and hogs and stealing gasoline, grain, antiques and alcohol. McElroy was indicted more than twenty times for various crimes, but when the cases came to trial, witnesses would withdraw. Many cited intimidation and threats by McElroy as the reason they wouldn't testify. In 1980, McElroy got into a confrontation with a seventy-year-old grocer because the man had caught one of McElroy's children stealing candy at the store. McElroy began stalking and making threats and, eventually, shot the man in the neck with a shotgun. Once again, McElroy was arrested and even convicted, but he got out on bail while waiting for an appeal. While he was out, he showed up at a local bar carrying a rifle and making threats against the life of the grocer (who had survived the earlier attack). After leaving the bar and getting in his car, a number of shots were fired. McElroy was hit with bullets from at least two different rifles and killed. No one called for an ambulance. There were more than forty people on the street or in a position to see what happened, but not one could describe the assailants.

Ken McElroy was killed in broad daylight in the public square with forty-six potential witnesses, and nobody saw anything. Nearly forty years have passed, and all sorts of investigations have taken place, but the crime is still unsolved. Perhaps there was a lot of confusion, and everyone in town just looked the wrong way. Or, maybe McElroy just found out the hard way that it was a bad idea to play chicken too many times with folks in a small town in the Outlaw State.

CASTLES AND COURTHOUSES

Toward the end of the nineteenth century, another phase in building seemed to take place in Missouri. Communities began building larger, more impressive courthouses. As city and county governments expanded their roles in daily lives, and as populations grew, more modern and impressive courthouses were built. With domed roofs and room for offices, some of these structures combined all law enforcement services in one building, including jail cells. The Buchanan County Courthouse in St. Joseph was one of the earlier versions of this style. Built in 1873, the jail and courthouse served to hold the Ford brothers as they faced trial for the murder of Jesse James. The Missouri counties' building phase, as it neared the end of the century, began to include prisons. County work farms and prisons began being placed away from residential areas and downtowns. The new facilities were made to house larger numbers of prisoners for longer periods of time. The day of the family hitching up the wagon and bringing a basket of food to a relative in the county jail had passed. Access was more strictly limited, and prisoners became more isolated from society. The day of the chain gang had not yet passed, and prison labor as a commodity was sold at a discount to local businesses in many jurisdictions. The use of prison labor was considered a way to reform and prepare inmates for life outside of prison.

In Kansas City, Missouri, the Vine Street Workhouse Castle was built in 1897. The design was prepared by prominent local architects A. Wallace Love and James Oliver Hog. The "castle," built in the Romanesque Revival style, calls to mind an ancient keep with towers and parapets. One expects to see a crossbowman or armored guard on the upper levels. Male prisoners worked for the Department of Public Works, while female prisoners housed at the facility were expected to make and mend prison uniforms. The castle/workhouse was in use until the 1920s. It then went

Buchanan County Courthouse and Jail, St. Joseph, Missouri. *Courtesy Library of Congress.*

Kansas City Missouri Workhouse Castle. *Author's collection.*

through several re-purposings until it was abandoned by the city in 1972. Attempts have been made to revive the old building, but it currently has brush growing around and inside of it and has a coat of graffiti on the lower levels. It is worth driving by during the day if you're visiting the Vine Street Historic District or downtown Kansas City.

8

OUTLAW CULTURE

In the middle of the nineteenth century, the United States of America was not united. It was divided economically, socially, geographically and politically and was being reconstituted from a multiplicity of cultures and races. It took a massive effort on the part of the two major political parties to pull the various groups into their camps for state and national elections. In the battle for history, writers had to build a national identity that a majority could accept. The dime novel and newspaper serials told exciting tales of the true men of the West. Ned Buntline had personally interviewed William Cody and wrote a serial and a play about "Buffalo Bill." He even wrote a play calling for Cody to play himself, *Scouts of the Plains*. Cody cut his teeth acting in Buntline's play, and no doubt the idea of his Wild West show came from seeing the packed crowds in New York and other eastern cities wanting to see the real thing. American ingenuity had finally figured out a way to sell the frontier experience without the risk and expense. Generations of city kids would grow up reading about Kit Carson, Wild Bill Hickok and Frank and Jesse James. Depicted in hundreds of serials, true detective books and Western dime novels—some while Jesse was still alive—the James brothers were a perennial favorite with readers and theatergoers. Cody not only appeared in plays and Western novels, but he also produced his own dime novels and toured his Wild West show across America and all over Europe. The show became so popular that dozens of imitators sprang up. Cole Younger and Frank James produced their own Wild West show after the turn of the century.

Puck cartoon lambasting dime novels. *Courtesy Library of Congress: LC-USZC2-1245.*

Right: William "Buffalo Bill" Cody. *Courtesy Library of Congress-LC-DIG-hec-03802.*

Below: Jesse James Western play poster, McSwain. *Courtesy Library of Congress: LC-USZ62-134779.*

Cole Younger. *Courtesy Library of Congress: LC-DIG-ggbain-21306.*

After the Civil War, former Confederate colonel George W. Miller moved to Newtonia, Missouri, and began seeking land in the Oklahoma Territory. He leased 110,000 acres from the Cherokee on which he started the 101 Ranch. Miller's ranch was successful, raising crops and cattle. His neighbor Gordon W. Lillie (a.k.a. "Pawnee Bill") had a successful Wild West show. In 1905, the 101 Ranch started its own show. While traveling with the show, Miller's sons had become interested in the fledgling film industry. In 1911, the Millers signed a contract with the New York Motion Picture Company and its subsidiary, the Bison Film Company. More than one hundred cowboys, cowgirls and Indians from the 101 show performed in movies for Bison. Several of the films were shot on location at the ranch. The idea of making Western films using real cowboys was probably born somewhere in New York. The 101 was a real working ranch; cowboys working there included Bill Pickett, Will Rogers and Tom Mix. Several of the hands on the 101 Ranch went on to have careers in film, including Tex Ritter, Jack Hoxie and Hoot Gibson. African American cowboy Bill Pickett was credited with inventing the rodeo sport of bulldogging and was featured showing his skills in a series of short films. Tom Mix was another working cowboy who was a skilled rodeo competitor turned entertainer. By shrewd marketing of Tom Mix movies and merchandise and the successful branding of Mix as a film and radio star, he was able to pull in a salary of $20,000 per week in the late 1920s. While in Hollywood, Mix became friends with Wyatt Earp, who lived there and sometimes worked as a consultant and even as an extra. At Wyatt Earp's funeral in 1929, movie stars William S. Hart and Tom Mix were among the pallbearers.

A big fan of the West and westerners, President Theodore Roosevelt became friends with former lawman Bat Masterson (who had come back East and was working as a sportswriter for the *New York Morning Telegraph*). Masterson, a frequent visitor to the White House, advised Roosevelt's press

Stagecoach holdup, Pawnee Bill Show. *Courtesy Library of Congress: LC-DIG-det-4a20068.*

101 show performer and movie actor Jack Hoxie, from *The Highwaymen. Courtesy Library of Congress: LC-USZ62-109397.*

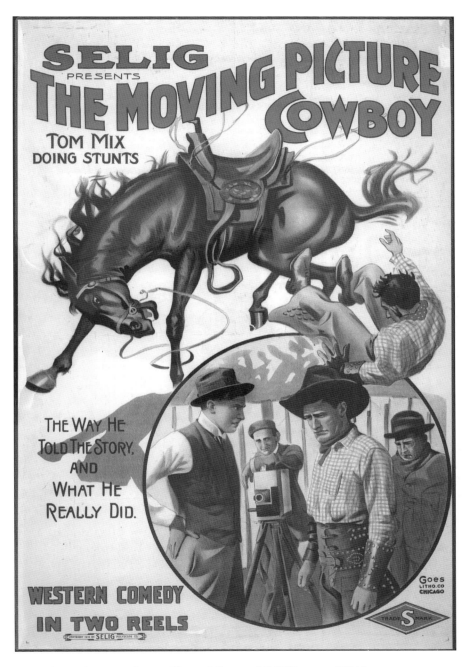

Tom Mix movie poster. *Courtesy Library of Congress*: LC-DIG-ppmsc-03513.

aide, Stuart Lake, that if he wanted to learn about the "real" west, he should talk to Wyatt Earp. Lake wrote *Wyatt Earp: Frontier Marshal* in 1931, and it was the basis for the movies *Frontier Marshal* with Randolph Scott and *My Darling Clementine* with Henry Fonda as Wyatt Earp. Another westerner turned movie actor with links to President Roosevelt was "Buffalo Bill" Cody. In 1894, William F. Cody starred in his first film, a short entitled *Buffalo Bill*. He would appear as himself in more than twenty documentaries and short films. He even garnered a producer credit for *The Indian Wars* (1914) and *The Adventures of Buffalo Bill* (1917). Jesse James Jr. starred in two films about his father, *Jesse James Under the Black Flag* and *Jesse James As the Outlaw*.

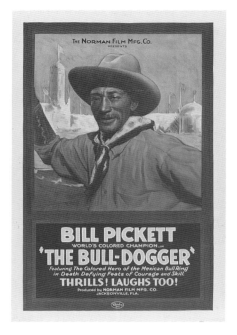

The Bull-Dogger movie poster (African American 101 Cowboy Bill Pickett). *Courtesy Wikimedia Commons.*

Train robber and leader of the Jennings Gang, Al Jennings, ended up in jail with the right cellmate. He shared his stories with fellow inmate and author William Sidney Porter (a.k.a. O. Henry). The acclaimed writer got out of prison first and appealed to President Roosevelt on Jennings's behalf. Jennings was released. In 1913, Al Jennings wrote *Beating Back*, a novel loosely based on his outlaw career. In it, he hit the same themes as other outlaws, casting himself as a skilled gunfighter and honorable man forced into a life of crime by corrupt lawmen. The *Saturday Evening Post* published a series of interviews with Jennings to coincide with the book release, and it became very successful. In 1908, Jennings re-created one of his crimes in *The Bank Robbery*, with famed lawman Heck Thomas acting as the posse leader and former U.S. deputy marshal Bill Tilghman serving as director. Jennings tried his hand at politics for a while but returned to writing, including *Through the Shadows with O. Henry* (1921) and film. He moved to Hollywood and ended up in twenty-four movies over the course of twenty-five years. Jennings lived to the ripe old age of ninety-eight.

Outlaw turned actor Al Jennings. *Courtesy Library of Congress: LC-DIG-npcc-10847.*

Emmett Dalton received more than twenty wounds in Coffeeville and lost two brothers. He served fourteen years in prison for his part in the attempted robbery of the two banks there. After leaving prison, Dalton went on tour in 1910, giving lectures on temperance and avoiding a life of crime. He also presented a film using some of the original and grisly photographs from the Coffeeville fiasco while talking about his outlaw life. Moving to Hollywood, he updated his film in 1912. The new production was called *The Last Stand of the Dalton Boys*. Dalton continued to work the lecture circuit, decrying the outlaw life while presenting films that reveled in it. He produced *Across the Chasm, When a Man's a Pal, The Man of the Desert* and another remake of his story, *Beyond the Law*. Dalton toured with *Beyond the Law* for seven years. In 1919, the *Kansas City Star* described him as a "movie magnate" who had stopped shooting people and started shooting movies. By 1922, he was president of the Standard Pictures Corporation, and by the 1930s, he was a wealthy man, having moved beyond film and into real estate.

One of the old outlaws who got into the movie business was Henry Starr, who starred in *A Debtor to the Law* in 1919 after serving several years in prison. Starr was twice sentenced to death by Judge Isaac Parker and managed to avoid the noose on technicalities both times. He started his career robbing banks and trains on horseback and claimed to have robbed more banks than the James brothers and the Doolin Gang combined (twenty-one, according to Starr). He served nearly half his life in prison for various crimes but was released more than once for being a model prisoner. When a member of the Cook Gang killed a prison guard with a smuggled gun, Starr volunteered to talk him down, with a promise that the guards wouldn't shoot him. Starr convinced the man to give up his gun. When he applied for parole, President Roosevelt was impressed with his courage and recommended a shortened sentence. In 1903, he was released. The next year, Henry's son Theodore Roosevelt Starr was born. Back in jail by 1908 for bank robbery, Henry was paroled in 1913 and, by 1914, had organized a new gang and went on an unmatched spree, robbing fourteen Oklahoma banks in five months. In March 1915, the gang, in an attempt to outdo the Daltons, succeeded in robbing two banks in Stroud, Oklahoma. Starr was wounded and left behind. He was then incarcerated again. Starr was a model prisoner and spoke out against his foolish crimes to the press. He was once again paroled in 1919 and produced his movie, which was a success. He was even offered the chance to make a film in Hollywood. Instead, Starr took the proceeds from the film and purchased a fast car and a machine pistol and went back to robbing banks. He was shot in the back while attempting to rob the People's State Bank in Harrison, Arkansas, in February 1921.

Every decade since the film industry began, one or more movies have been made to retell the story of Frank and Jesse James, more than eighty films in all. *The James Boys in Missouri* (1908) and *Jesse James* (1911) got the ball rolling with the basic dime novel versions of the story. A more sympathetic portrayal followed when Jesse James Jr. played the part of his father in *Jesse James Under the Black Flag* (1921) and *Jesse James the Outlaw* (1922). In the 1930s, there was *Jesse James* (1930) and another *Jesse James* (1939), in which the popular

Tyrone Power played Jesse and Henry Fonda played Frank. *Days of Jesse James* appeared in 1939. In the 1940s, there were a dozen films produced about the James brothers, including *The Return of Frank James*, with Henry Fonda playing the lead character (1940), *Jesse James at Bay* (1941) and *Jesse James Rides Again* (1947), the latter starring as Jesse the man who would become famous for playing the Lone Ranger: Clayton Moore. Many of these films introduced other guerrillas, such as the Youngers, Quantrill, Bloody Bill and even Arch Clement. In the 1950s, another dozen films about the James brothers were made. *Kansas Raiders* (1950) starred war hero Audie Murphy as a morally torn Jesse being led astray by bad man William Quantrill. Don "Red" Barry (the original Red Ryder) starred,

A Debtor to the Law. Courtesy Wikimedia Commons.

co-wrote, coproduced and directed the fiction "classic" *Jesse James' Women* (1954). One advertising poster shows two women wrestling and pulling each other's hair and has the taglines "The Battle of the Sexes and the Sixes Rages Across the Lusty West" and "Women wanted him…more than the law!" The poster for *Jesse James vs. the Daltons* (1954) touts, "The Fastest gun of the West—against the deadliest gang of all!" But the title is a misnomer; the lead character is believed to be Jesse's son. (At least the film was in 3-D.) Rounding out the decade, *The True Story of Jesse James* (1957) starred Robert Wagner as Jesse and (I can't resist) Alan Hale Jr. (Skipper from *Gilligan's Island*) as Cole Younger and, last but not least, *Alias Jesse James* (1959) starred comedian Bob Hope as an inept insurance agent who sells Jesse a $100,000 policy—nonsense soon follows.

In the 1960s, the portrayals of the James Gang ran the gamut from the made-for-television *"Bronco" Shadow of Jesse James* (1960), in which James Coburn plays Jesse as a heartless killer, to *Jesse James Meets Frankenstein's Daughter* (1965), in which Jesse and wounded gang member Hank Tracy show up at the castle of Baron Frankenstein's granddaughter, who transforms Hank into a monster she names Igor. (This film was followed up in 1966 with *Billy the Kid vs. Dracula*.) Even the Three Stooges got in on the act with the release of *The Outlaws Is Coming* (1965), in which they have run-ins with Jesse James, Wyatt Earp and Wild Bill Hickok while working out West. In the 1970s, a grittier style of Western emerged, *The Great Northfield Minnesota Raid* (1972) was bloody and earthy; Robert Duvall portrayed Jesse as mentally unstable and cruel. A fictional portrayal of a Missouri outlaw was presented in *The Outlaw Josey Wales* (1976), and it was in many ways more historically accurate and balanced than dozens of its predecessors. In the 1980s, several attempts to tell the story more accurately were made. *The Long Riders* (1980) went so far as to cast sets of acting brothers to play the gang members. The three Carradine brothers (David, Keith and Robert) played the three Youngers (Cole, Jim and Bob); the Keach brothers (James and Stacy) played Jesse and Frank James; and Dennis and Randy Quaid played Ed and Clell Miller, respectively. In the 1990s, a few more films about the brothers were added to the list, though these were again eclipsed by a fictional yet more compelling treatment of the guerrillas in *Ride with the Devil* (1999). A number of documentaries rounded out the filmography as the new millennium

Jesse James (1939). *Courtesy Wikimedia Commons.*

Jesse James' Women. Courtesy Wikimedia Commons.

began. In *The Assassination of Jesse James by the Coward Robert Ford* (2007), actor Brad Pitt (raised in Springfield and attended the University of Missouri) plays out the last part of Jesse's life, with the distrust and sense of impending doom that must have hung over a man who had been on the run half his life but never strayed long or far from home.

The full filmography of every Missouri outlaw or lawman would be enormous. Belle Starr was played by Gene Tierney (*Belle Starr*, 1941) and Jane Russell (*Montana Belle*, 1952). Calamity Jane was portrayed by Doris Day (*Calamity Jane*, 1953), William Quantrill was portrayed by veteran actor Brian Donlevy (*Kansas Raiders*, 1950) and by ex-convict turned character actor Leo Gordon (*Quantrill's Raiders*, 1958). And the list doesn't end with the movies. There have been countless songs recorded by artists from Bob Dylan to Emmylou Harris about the outlaws. Television shows from the Twilight Zone to the Brady Bunch paid homage to the Jesse James legend (not to mention *Little House on the Prairie*, *The Simpsons*, *My Favorite Martian* and *The Dukes of Hazzard*). There are comic-book versions of the story and Japanese manga characters based on the old outlaws. In the video game

Senator Harry Truman and Vice President John Nance Garner looking at guns once owned by Jesse James. *Courtesy Library of Congress: LC-DIG-hec-29118.*

Bill and Ted's Excellent Video Game Adventure, the characters must give an Uzi (machine gun) to Jesse James.

Woven into the fabric of our culture is a fascination with the frontier and the simple stories of good and evil battling it out with bigger-than-life backgrounds and music. We drive Broncos and Silverados and eat Log Cabin Syrup and Tombstone Pizza. We cheer for the Dallas Cowboys, the Washington Redskins or the Cleveland Indians and in dozens of other ways are influenced by packaged and marketed versions of real people who, somewhere in our inner selves, we want to be like. Not that the average person wants to live the outlaw life. Rather, the average person craves the outlaw's courage and respects his commitment to a life of excitement, danger and independence. The fantasy of thumbing your nose at the wealthy and powerful is a satisfying one. In Jesse James, Missouri gave America its Robin Hood and, along with Harry Truman, a pair of straight-talking, straight-shooting cultural icons...whom you wouldn't want to play chicken with.

BIBLIOGRAPHY

Barile, Mary Collins. *The Santa Fe Trail in Missouri*. Columbia: University of Missouri Press, 2010.

Barton, O.S. *Three Years with Quantrill—A True Story Told by His Scout John McCorkle*. With notes by Albert Castel and commentary by Herman Hattaway. Norman: University of Oklahoma Press, 1992.

Brown, A. Theodore. *Frontier Community: Kansas City to 1870*. Columbia: University of Missouri Press, 1963.

Brownlee, Richard S. *Gray Ghosts of the Confederacy: Guerrilla Warfare in the West, 1961–1865*. Baton Rouge: Louisiana State University Press, 1958.

Castel, Albert. *A Frontier State at War: Kansas 1861–1865*. Lawrence, KS: Heritage Press, 1958. For the American Historical Society. New material by Edward E. Leslie, 1992.

———. *General Sterling Price and the Civil War in the West*. Baton Rouge: Louisiana State University Press, 1968.

Davis, Dale E. "Guerrilla Operations in the Civil War: Assessing Compound Warfare During Price's Raid." Master's thesis, U.S. Army Command and General Staff College, 2004.

Dyer, Robert L. *Jesse James and the Civil War in Missouri*. Columbia: University of Missouri Press, 1994.

Edwards, John N. *Noted guerrillas, or The warfare of the border: being a history of the lives and adventures of Quantrell, Bill Anderson, George Todd, David Poole, Fletcher Taylor, Peyton Long, Oll Shepherd, Arch Clements, John Maupin, Tuck and Woot Hill, Wm. Gregg, Thomas Maupin, the James brothers, the Younger brothers, Arthur McCoy and numerous other well known guerrillas of the West*. St. Louis, MO: Bryan Brand 1887.

Faragher, John Mack. *Daniel Boone: The Life and Legend of an American Pioneer*. New York: Henry Holt & Company, 1992.

Faulkner, William. *Intruder in the Dust*. New York: Random House, 1948.

Foley, William E. *The Genesis of Missouri: From Wilderness Outpost to Statehood*. Columbia: University of Missouri Press, 1989.

————. *A History of Missouri*. Vol. 1, *1673 to 1820*. William E. Parrish, general editor. Columbia: University of Missouri Press, [1971] 2000.

Goodrich, Thomas. *Black Flag: Guerrilla Warfare on the Western Border, 1861–1865*. Bloomington: Indiana University Press, 1995.

Hurt, R. Douglas. *Nathan Boone and the American Frontier*. Columbia: University of Missouri Press, 1998.

Jackson, David W., and Paul Kirkman. *Lockdown: Outlaws, Lawmen, & Frontier Justice in Jackson County, Missouri*. Independence, MO: Two Trails Publishing for Jackson County Historical Society, 2009.

James, Jesse, Jr. *Jesse James, My Father*. Cleveland, OH: Buckeye Publishing Company, 1899.

Jones, Mary Ellen. *The American Frontier: Opposing Viewpoints*. San Diego, CA: Greenhaven Press, 1994.

Kansas City Star. "Own a Wild West Show." February 18, 1903.

Bibliography

———. "Pendergast Sworn In." December 22, 1902.

———. "Wild West Show Starts." May 8, 1903.

Levens, Henry C., and Nathaniel M. Drake. *A History of Cooper County, Missouri*. St. Louis, MO: Perrin & Smith, Steam Book and Job Printers, 1876.

McCandless, Perry. *A History of Missouri*. Vol. 2, *1820–1860*. Columbia: University of Missouri Press, 1972, 1987.

Morgan, Robert *Boone: A Biography*. Chapel Hill, NC, Algonquin Books, 2007.

Munkres, Robert L. "Crime on the Oregon Trail: 1838–1864." *Tombstone Epitaph*, March, 1995.

Odessan (Odessa, MO). "The Durbin Gang, Lafayette County's Infamous Train Robbers." June 4, 2009.

Pace, J. Brradley. *Survivors: A Catalog of Missouri's Remaining 19th Century Courthouses*. CreateSpace Independent Publishing Platform, March 14, 2012.

Rowe, Mary Ellen. *Bulwark of the Republic: The American Militia in Antebellum West*. Westport, CT: Praeger, 2003.

Smith, Robert Barr. *The Outlaws: Tales of Bad Guys Who Shaped the Wild West*. Guilford, CT: Twodot, 2013.

Steele, Philip W., and Steve Cotrell. *Civil War in the Ozarks*. Gretna, LA: Pelican Publishing, 1993.

Steward, Dick. *The Life and Legend of John Smith T*. Columbia: University of Missouri Press, 2000.

Ward, Stephanie Francis. "The Lawyer Who Took On Jesse James…and Won." *ABA Journal* (March 2008.)

Wellman, Paul I. *A Dynasty of Western Outlaws*. Lincoln: University of Nebraska Press, 1986.

Wood, Larry. *Desperadoes of the Ozarks*. Gretna, LA: Pelican Publishing, 2011.

INDEX

ABOUT THE AUTHOR

Paul Kirkman is the author of *The Battle of Westport: Missouri's Great Confederate Raid* (The History Press, 2011) and *Forgotten Tales of Kansas City* (The History Press, 2012) and is the coauthor (with David Jackson) of *Lockdown: Outlaws, Lawmen, and Frontier Justice in Jackson County, Missouri* (Jackson County Historical Society, 2012). Paul has a BA in history from Columbia College and is a speaker with Show Me Missouri: Conversations about Missouri's Past, Present, and Future; a speakers' bureau program jointly organized and managed by the Missouri Humanities Council and the State Historical Society of Missouri. He lives in Independence, Missouri, with his wife, Shawn, and his daughter Shannon.

Visit us at
www.historypress.net